WORLD'S GREA
CHRISTMAS SONGS

for Easy Piano and Voice with Optional Chord Symbols for Guitar

65 of the World's Most Popular and Best Loved

Traditional and Contemporary Christmas Songs

Revised Edition

Selected and Arranged by
DAN FOX

You'll sound great when you sit at the keyboard with this fantastic collection of Christmas songs. All of the old favorites are here: *Silent Night*; *Jingle Bells*; *Angels We Have Heard on High*; *Deck the Hall*; *Joy to the World*; *O Come, All Ye Faithful (Adeste Fideles)*; *The Twelve Days of Christmas*; *God Rest Ye Merry, Gentlemen* . . . the list goes on and on.

But we have also included many popular songs about Christmas: modern classics like *Feliz Navidad*, *Home for the Holidays*, *Believe* (Josh Groban's great hit from "The Polar Express"), *Where Are You Christmas* (Faith Hill's smash from "How the Grinch Stole Christmas"), *A Marshmallow World*, *Winter Wonderland*, *Santa Claus Is Comin' to Town*, *Let It Snow! Let It Snow! Let It Snow!*, *I'll Be Home for Christmas* and many, many more.

And we haven't forgotten the children! They'll find *Rudolph, the Red-Nosed Reindeer, Frosty the Snowman, Nuttin' for Christmas*, and *The Little Drummer Boy*. You'll smile when you play *All I Want for Christmas Is My Two Front Teeth* and *Grandma Got Run Over by a Reindeer*. You'll rock with *Rockin' Around the Christmas Tree* and *Jingle Bell Rock*, and to welcome in the New Year after the holiday season *Auld Lang Syne* is included.

Each song contains the complete words, music, and chord symbols in a fully fingered, easy-to-play, professional sounding arrangement. Even Santa couldn't ask for anything more!

Copyright © MMVIII by Alfred Publishing Co., Inc.
All rights reserved.   Printed in USA.
ISBN-10: 0-7390-5585-2
ISBN-13: 978-0-7390-5585-4

CONTENTS

Bandleader Spike Jones was famous for parodying dozens of "serious" songs by using gunshots, screams, squeaks, gurgles, gargles and other noises to hilarious effect. In 1948, he and his band, The City Slickers, had a big hit with this song, unforgettably sung by chubby lead trumpeter George Rock, wearing short pants with his two front teeth blacked out.

ALL I WANT FOR CHRISTMAS IS MY TWO FRONT TEETH

Words and Music by
Don Gardner

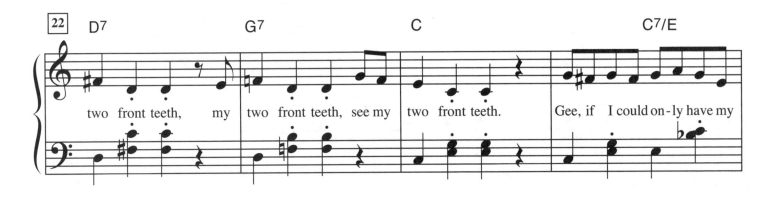

No one knows who wrote this beautiful carol. It was first published in the late 18th century in translation from a book called *Musical and Poetical Relicks of the Welsh Bards.* Since then the original poem has been modified many times, but this version is the best known.

ALL THROUGH THE NIGHT

Traditional Welsh Carol

1. Sleep, my Child, and peace at-tend Thee all through the night.
2. While the moon her watch is keep-ing all through the night;
3. You, my God, a Babe of won-der all through the night;

Guard-ian an-gels God will send Thee all through the night.
While the wear-y world is sleep-ing all through the night.
Dreams you dream can't break from thun-der all through the night.

Soft the drow-sy hours are creep-ing, Hill and vale in slum-ber sleep-ing,
Through your dreams you're swift-ly steal-ing, Vis-ions of de-light re-veal-ing,
Chil-dren's dreams can-not be bro-ken, Life is but a love-ly to-ken.

God His lov-ing vig-il keep-ing all through the night.
Christ-mas time is so ap-peal-ing all through the night.
Christ-mas should be soft-ly spo-ken all through the night.

By the end of the 1920s, most American families had access to a radio, which became the focus of family evenings at home. At midnight on the last day of 1929, the popular orchestra of Guy Lombardo and His Royal Canadians broadcast their tremulous version of "Auld Lang Syne." Since then, the song has been obligatory on New Year's Eve. Strangely, little is known about its origins. The Scottish poet Robert Burns is given credit for some of the verses, but the first and best-known verse, as well as the music, are of unknown authorship. The title means "old times' sake."

AULD LANG SYNE

Words by Robert Burns
Music: Traditional Scottish Melody

One of the most popular carols of all time, this one comes from several sources. The melody of the first part is derived from an 18th-century popular song. The words are a translation of a French Carol, *Les anges dans nos campagnes (Angels in Our Countryside)*. The famous refrain, "Gloria in excelsis Deo" is thought to date from the Middle Ages. The carol was first published in its present form in 1855.

ANGELS WE HAVE HEARD ON HIGH

Joyously

Traditional

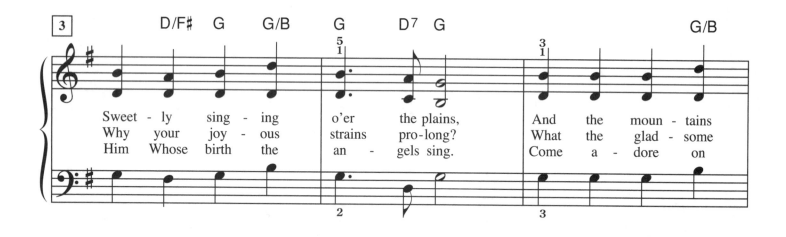

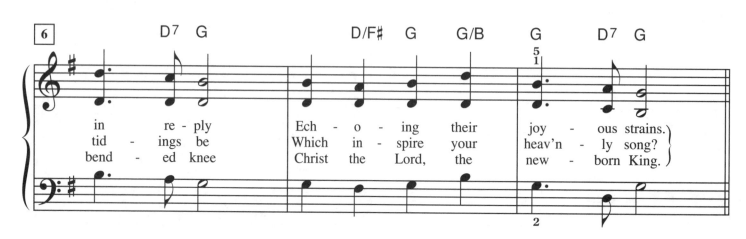

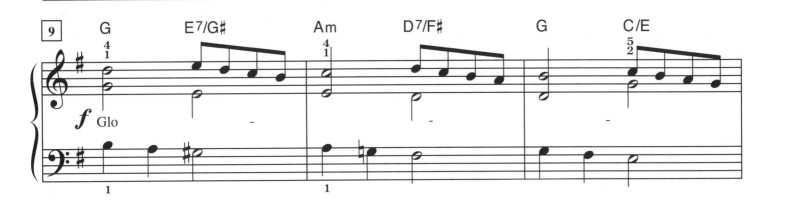

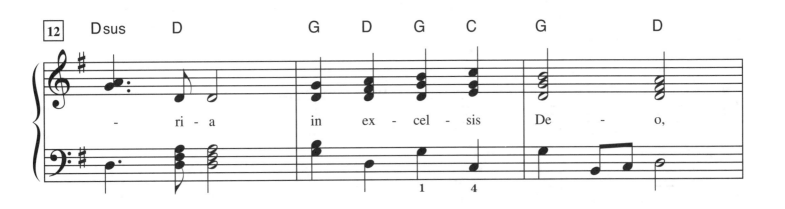

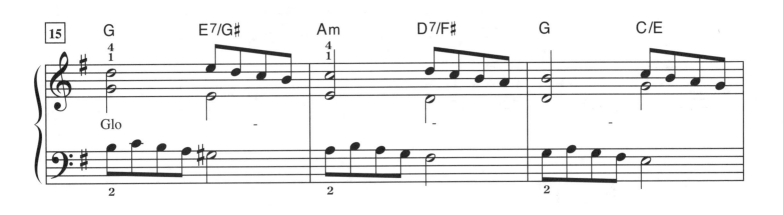

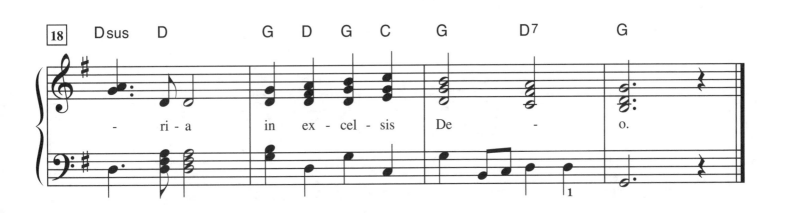

Undoubtedly the most popular of Tchaikovsky's ballets, *The Nutcracker* is still performed in dozens, perhaps hundreds of venues throughout the world every Christmastime. Although Russian composer Peter Ilyich Tchaikovsky (1840–1893) lived an anxiety-ridden and tortured life, there's no trace of depression or sadness in the music for this ballet, a children's favorite.

ARABIAN DANCE
(FROM *THE NUTCRACKER*)

Music by
Peter Ilyich Tchaikovsky

James Murray first published this children's carol in his *Dainty Songs for Little Lads and Lasses* in 1887. He called it "Luther's Cradle Hymn" (supposedly composed by Martin Luther for his children). However, there is no evidence that Martin Luther had anything to do with it, and most authorities now believe that Murray himself wrote the music.

Away in a Manger

Words: Anonymous (stanzas 1, 2)
John Thomas McFarland (stanza 3)
Music by James R. Murray

In 1985, multi-talented Chris Van Allsburg wrote and illustrated *The Polar Express*, a best-selling children's Christmas book about holding onto the faith of childhood. In 2004 the magical tale was turned into a highly successful film starring Tom Hanks. To retain the sweet, nostalgic quality of the book's illustrations, the filmmakers used "capture technology," which uses live actors to create animated characters. This song, sung by Josh Groban, was the hit of the film.

Believe
(FROM "THE POLAR EXPRESS")

Words and Music by
Alan Silvestri and Glenn Ballard

1. Chil - dren___ sleep - ing,___ snow is soft - ly fall - ing.___
2. Trains move_ quick - ly___ to their jour - ney's end._____

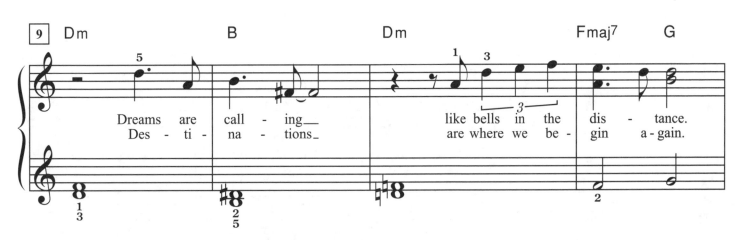

Dreams are call - ing___ like bells in the dis - tance.
Des - ti - na - tions_ are where we be - gin a - gain.

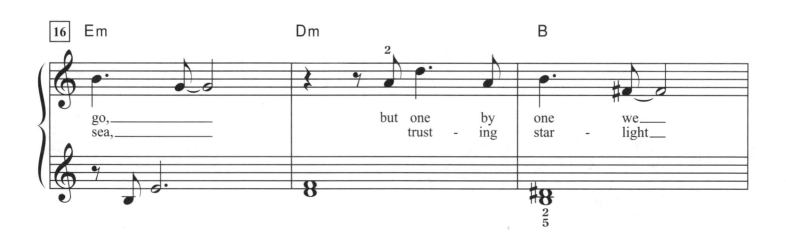

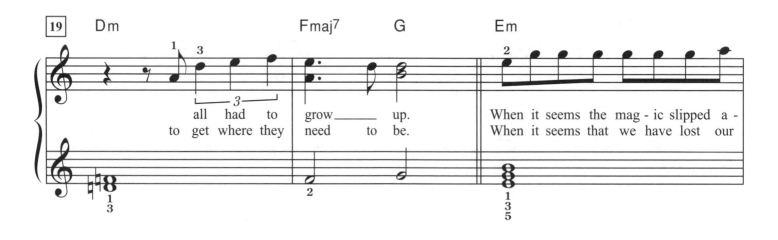

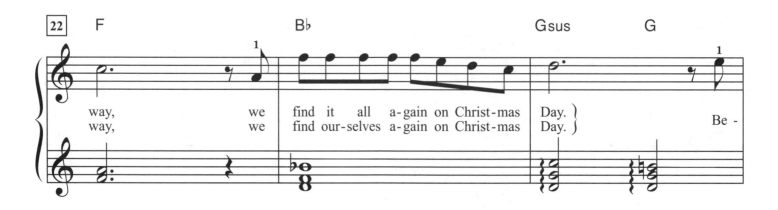

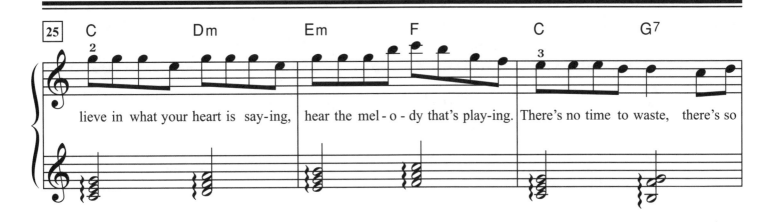

lieve in what your heart is say-ing, hear the mel - o - dy that's play-ing. There's no time to waste, there's so

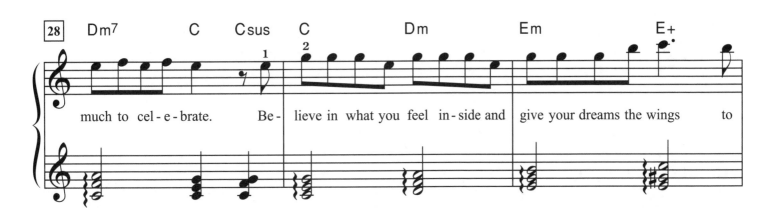

much to cel - e - brate. Be - lieve in what you feel in - side and give your dreams the wings to

fly. You have ev - 'ry-thing you need if you just

1. C ... be - lieve.

2. C ... be - lieve.

Similar to the old tearjerker, "M-O-T-H-E-R," this song also uses each letter of its spelled-out title as inspiration for the lyrics that follow. This song has a simple melody with heartfelt lyrics, and recordings of the piece became hits for country music stars Eddy Arnold and Jim Reeves.

C-H-R-I-S-T-M-A-S

Words and Music by
Eddy Arnold and Jenny Lou Carson

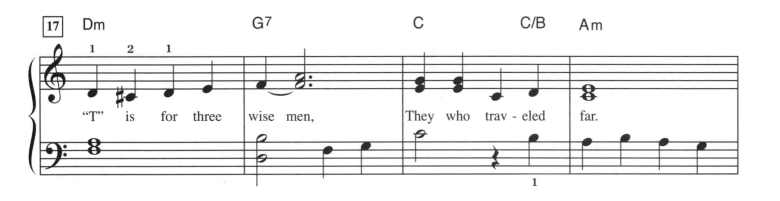

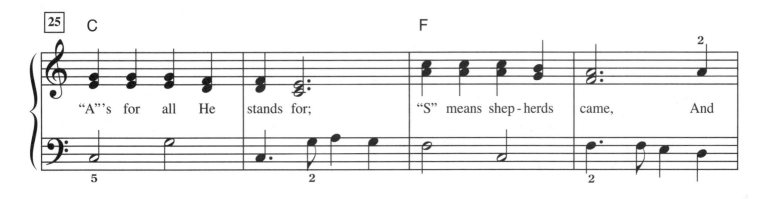

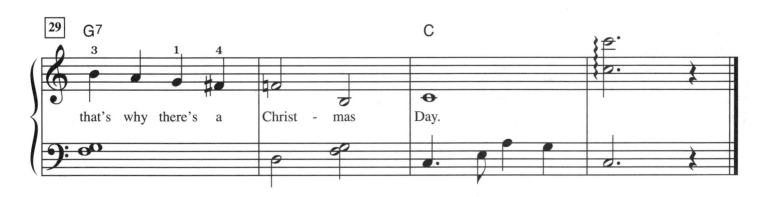

The idea of setting a Christmas song to the rhythm of an Irish jig occurred to three Irish songwriters back in the 1950s. They came up with this spirited song, which became a big hit for Irish tenor Dennis Day in 1951. Killarney is a lovely town in the southwest part of Ireland.

CHRISTMAS IN KILLARNEY

Words and Music by
John Redmond, James Cavanaugh
and Frank Weldon

neigh-bors pay a call. And Fa - ther John be-fore he's gone will bless the house and all. How

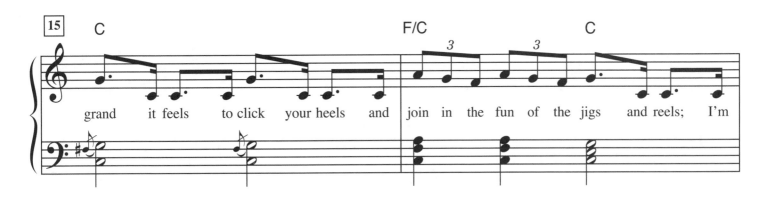

grand it feels to click your heels and join in the fun of the jigs and reels; I'm

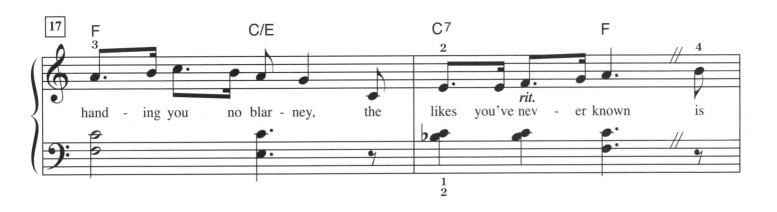

hand - ing you no blar - ney, the likes you've nev - er known is

Christ-mas in Kil-lar-ney with all of the folks at home. The all of the folks at home.

If you were to compile a list of the best-loved Christmas songs written in the last 50 years or so, this one would be on most everyone's list. Written by crooner Mel Tormé (The Velvet Fog) and his friend Robert Wells, the song evokes heartwarming images of the things we associate with the holiday season. Nat Cole's creamy-smooth rendition, recorded in 1946, has established the song as a Christmas perennial.

THE CHRISTMAS SONG
(CHESTNUTS ROASTING ON AN OPEN FIRE)

Lyric and Music by
Mel Tormé and Robert Wells

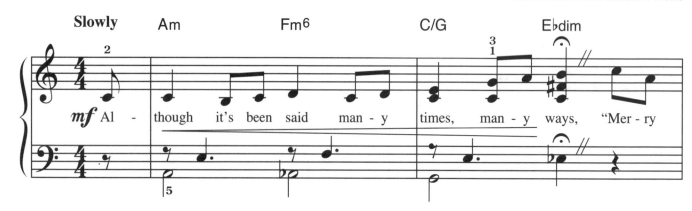

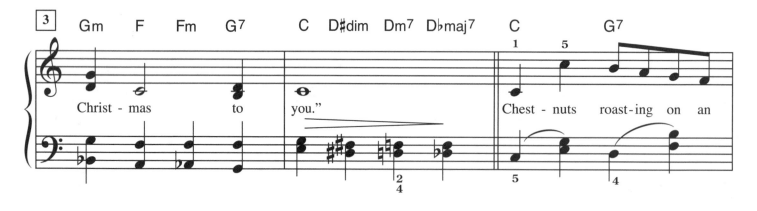

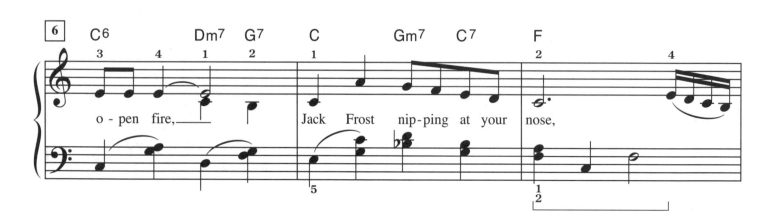

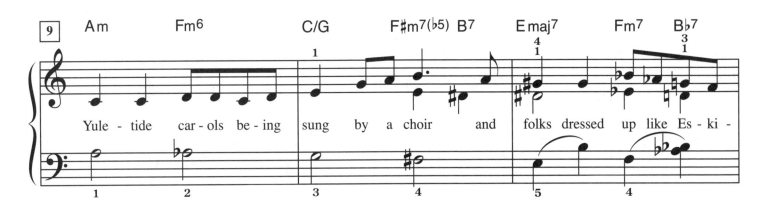

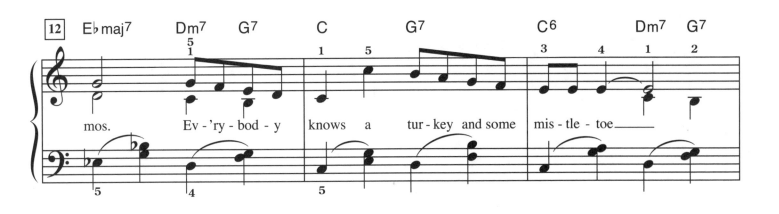

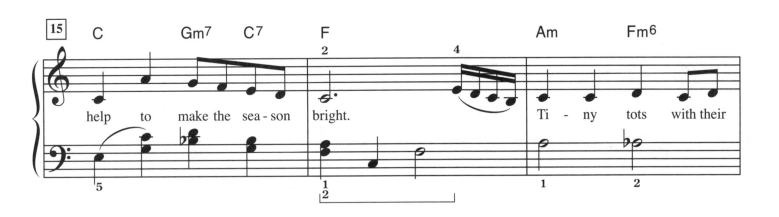

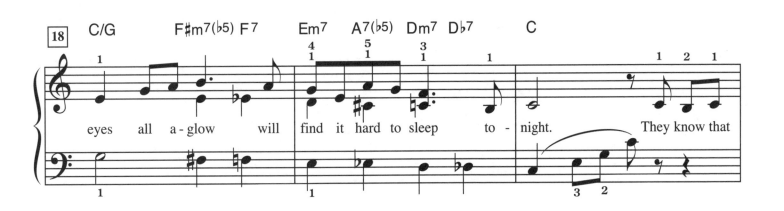

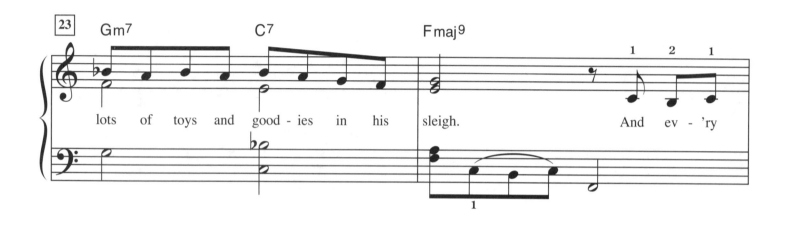

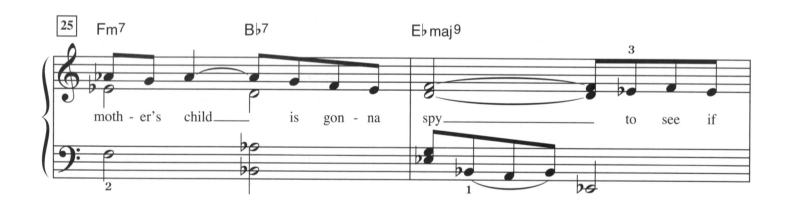

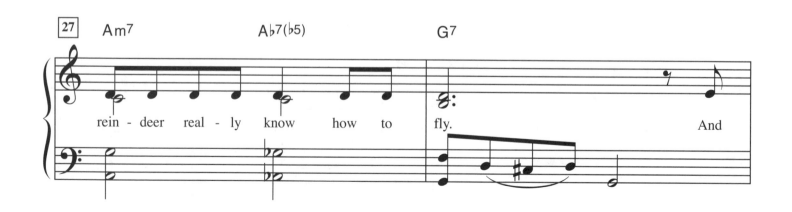

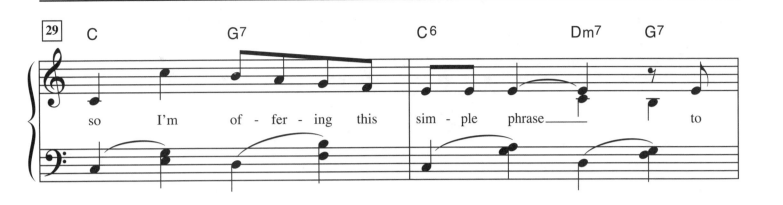

29 C   G7   C6   Dm7   G7

so   I'm   of - fer - ing   this   sim - ple   phrase____   to

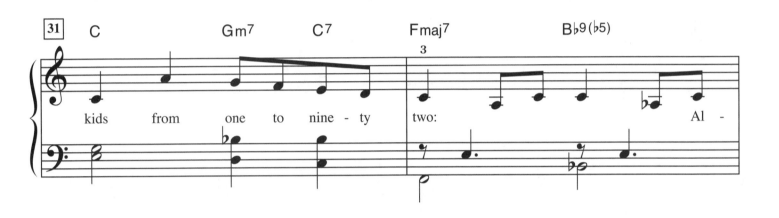

31 C   Gm7   C7   Fmaj7   B♭9(♭5)

kids   from   one   to   nine - ty   two: Al -

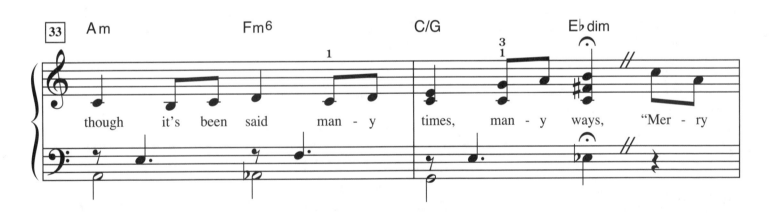

33 Am   Fm6   C/G   E♭dim

though   it's   been   said   man - y   times,   man - y   ways,   "Mer - ry

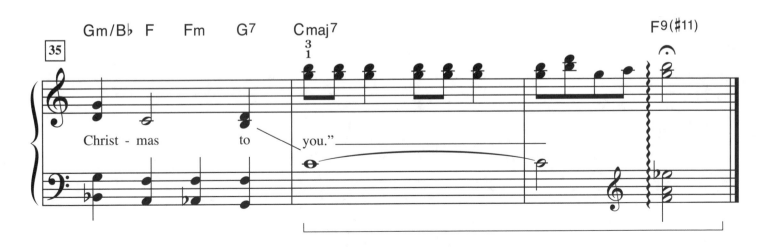

Gm/B♭   F   Fm   G7   Cmaj7   F9(♯11)

35

Christ - mas   to   you."____

The songwriting team of Sammy Kahn and Jule Styne was responsible for innumerable hit songs. Among these hits are "Three Coins in the Fountain," "I'll Walk Alone," jazz standard "Time After Time," and "Let It Snow! Let It Snow! Let It Snow!" (on page 84). This piece dates from 1954 and was written at the request of Frank Sinatra.

THE CHRISTMAS WALTZ

Words by Sammy Cahn
Music by Jule Styne

John Francis Wade was an Englishman who lived in France in the 18th century. He is credited as the author of both the Latin words and the melody of this beloved hymn; however, some authorities believe the melody predates Wade. Frederick Oakeley, a Catholic priest who eventually became Canon of Westminster, translated the words into English in 1852.

O Come, All Ye Faithful
(ADESTE FIDELES)

Latin words by John Francis Wade
English translation by Frederick Oakeley
Music by John Francis Wade

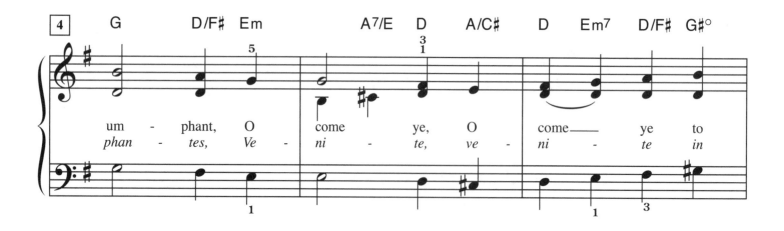

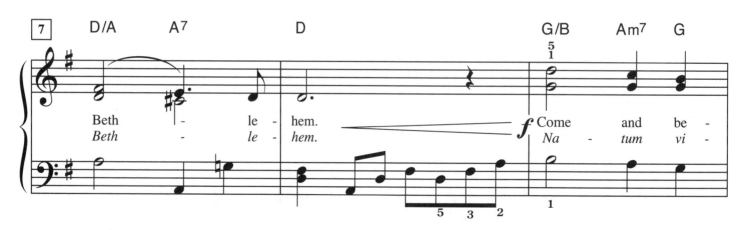

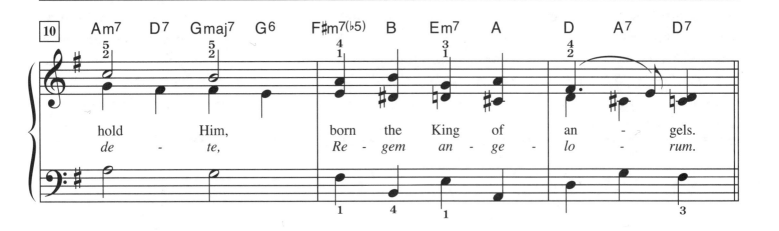

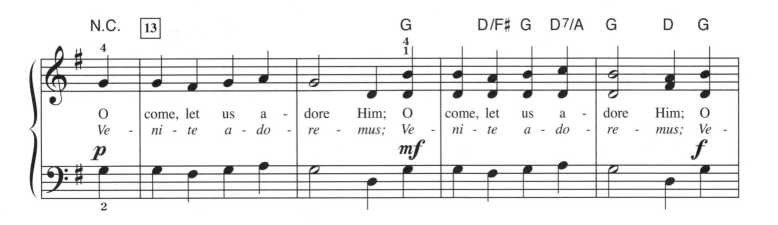

2. Sing, choirs of angels,
   Sing in exultation;
   Sing all ye citizens of heav'n above.
   Glory to God, all glory in the highest.
   O come, let us adore Him;
   O come, let us adore Him;
   O come, let us adore Him, Christ, the Lord.

3. Yea, Lord, we greet Thee,
   Born this happy morning;
   Jesus, to Thee be all glory giv'n;
   Word of the Father, now in flesh appearing.
   O come, let us adore Him;
   O come, let us adore Him;
   O come, let us adore Him, Christ, the Lord.

Millions of people revere the serenely beautiful melodies originally called Latin plainsong. These chants date back to a time before music had accompanying chords, a steady beat, or any kind of definite notation. Plainsong was already ancient when Pope (later Saint) Gregory had hundreds of them written down about 1,500 years ago. In his honor we call them Gregorian chants. The music of this carol is plainsong, but over the years, writers and arrangers have added modern chords, measured notation and a lovely set of English words. Emmanuel, a poetic name for Jesus, comes from the Hebrew "God is with us."

O Come, O Come, Emmanuel

English lyrics by John M. Neale
13th-century Plainsong

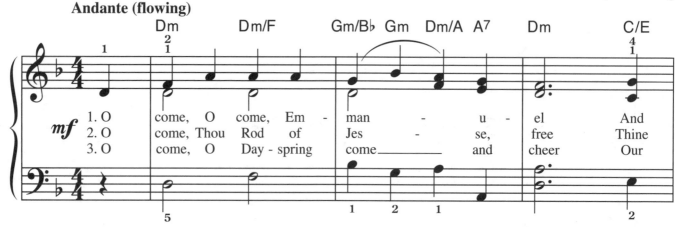

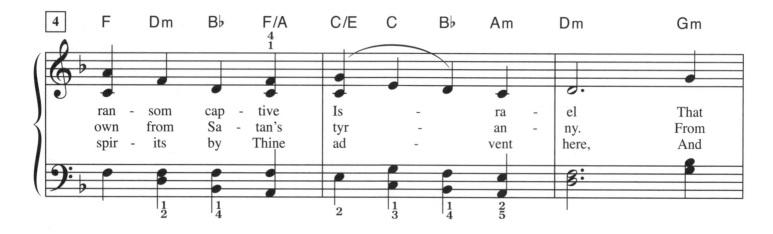

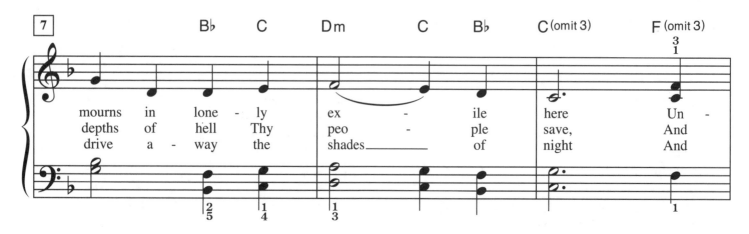

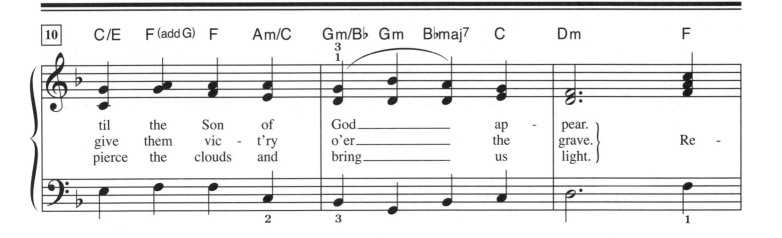

til the Son of God _____ ap - pear.
give them vic - t'ry o'er _____ the grave.
pierce the clouds and bring _____ us light. Re -

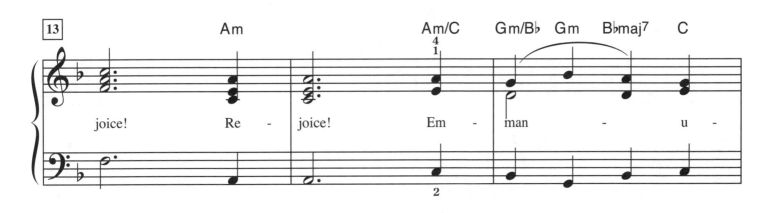

joice! Re - joice! Em - man - u -

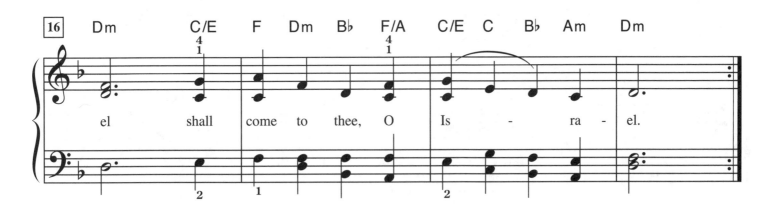

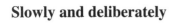

el shall come to thee, O Is - ra - el.

Slowly and deliberately

Decorating a Christmas tree at holiday time was originally a German practice, but in the last 200 or so years, the custom has spread all over the world. The melody of *O Christmas Tree* is an old German folk song, first published in 1799. Subsequently, many sets of words have been written for this tune, including the college song "Lauriger Horatius" and the great rallying song of the Confederacy "Maryland, My Maryland."

O CHRISTMAS TREE
(O TANNENBAUM)

Traditional German Carol

Before Christianity reached Britain, pagan tribes had long been decorating their dwellings with holly boughs as a protection against evil spirits. With the arrival of Christianity the tradition continued, with the holly symbolizing Christ's death and resurrection. Even today the holly's red berries and green leaves are the traditional colors of the holiday. The original Welsh words were about New Year's night; the familiar American words printed here date from the 1880s.

DECK THE HALL

Traditional Welsh Carol

Jose Feliciano was born in Puerto Rico in 1945. Blind from birth, Jose worked hard and became a highly successful singer/guitarist and songwriter. This song, which was the title of his 1970 album, ranks among the 25 most-performed Christmas songs in the world.

Feliz Navidad

Words and Music by José Feliciano

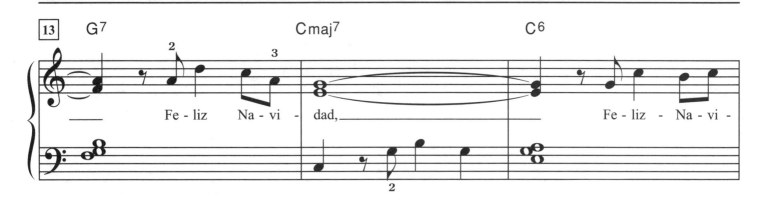

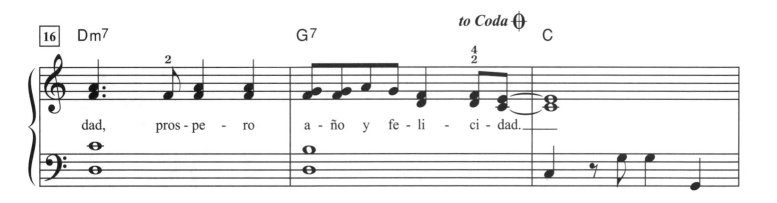

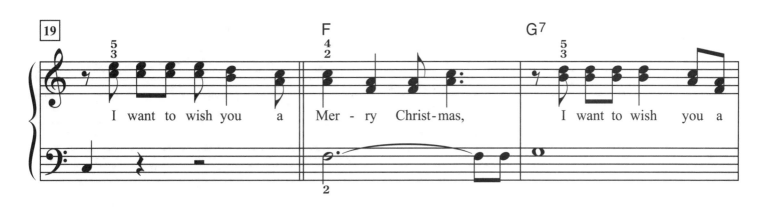

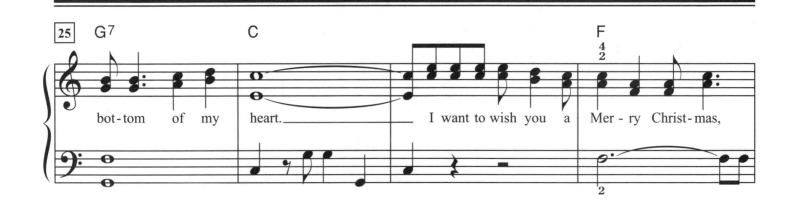

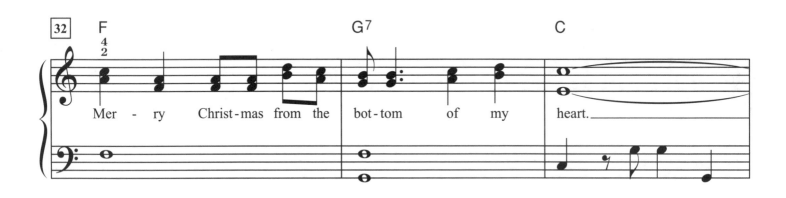

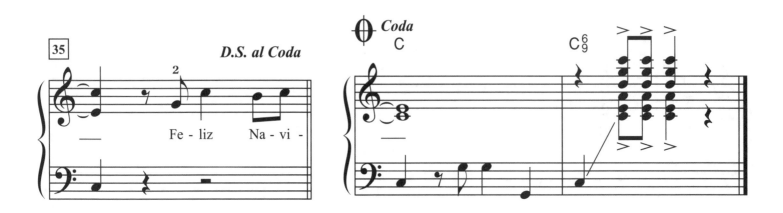

Surely one of the most popular children's Christmas songs ever written, Frosty first appeared as a story, then as a television special that featured this song. Actor/comedian Jimmy Durante made his last appearance as the narrator of this animated special. Songwriters Steve Nelson and Jack Rollins perfectly captured the fun and magic of a snowman who comes to life, even if only briefly.

FROSTY THE SNOWMAN

Words and Music by
Steve Nelson and Jack Rollins

Moderately bright

1. Frost - y the Snow-man was a jol - ly, hap - py soul, With a
2. Frost - y the Snow-man knew the sun was hot that day, So he

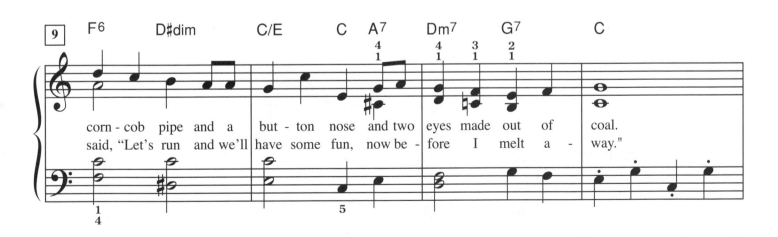

corn - cob pipe and a but - ton nose and two eyes made out of coal.
said, "Let's run and we'll have some fun, now be - fore I melt a - way."

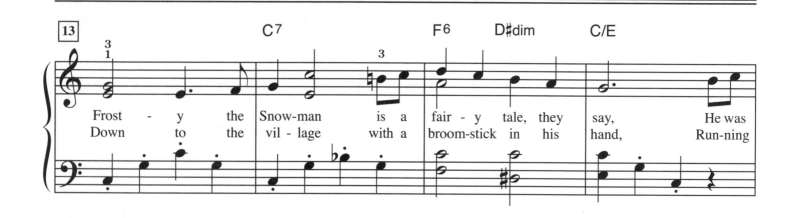

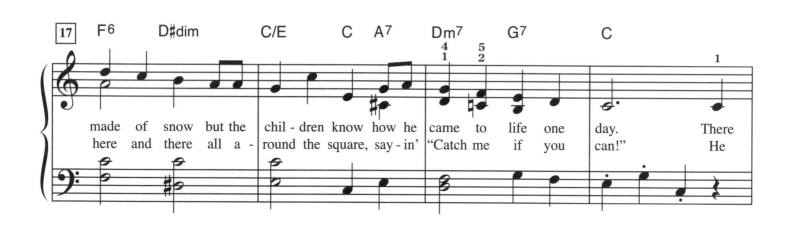

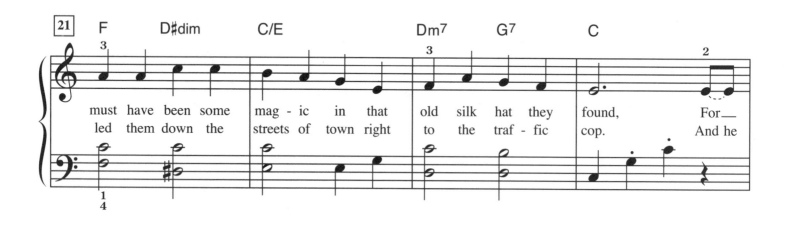

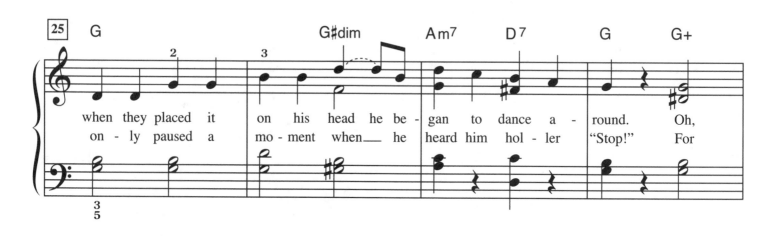

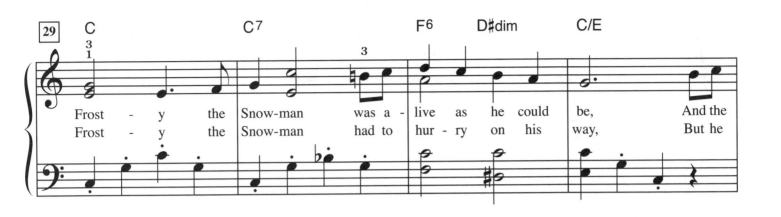

Frost - y the Snow-man was a - live as he could be, And the
Frost - y the Snow-man had to hur - ry on his way, But he

chil - dren say he could laugh and play just the same as you and me.
waved good - bye say-in' "Don't you cry, I'll be back a - gain some day."

Thump-et-y thump thump, thump-et-y thump thump, look at Frost - y go;

Thump-et-y thump thump, thump-et-y thump thump O - ver the hills of snow.

Noël is the French word for Christmas. On *la nuit avant Noël* (the night before Christmas) French children wait for *Bonhomme Noël* (Old Man Christmas) who leaves toys and sweets on the hearth for children who have been good. For the naughty ones, bogeyman *Père Fouettard* leaves a bundle of switches for punishment. The first complete version of this carol in English dates from 1833.

THE FIRST NOEL

Traditional

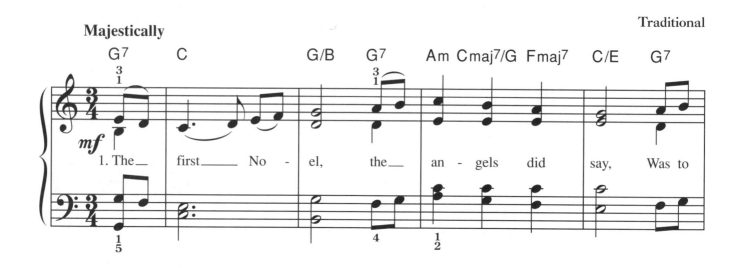

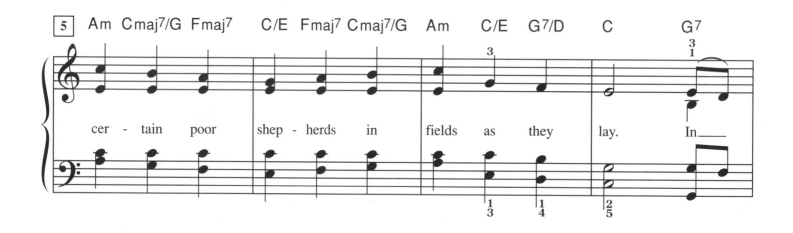

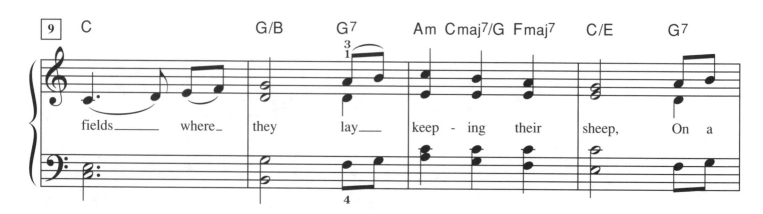

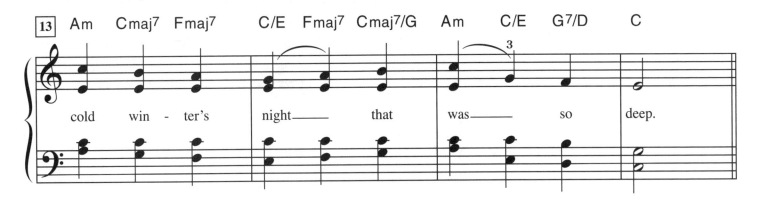

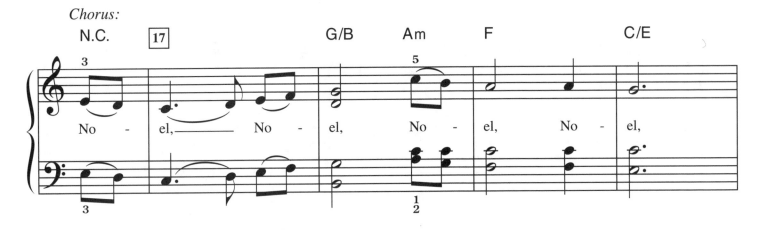

Chorus:

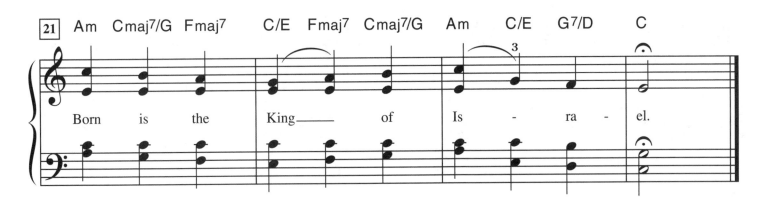

2. They looked up and saw a star,
   Shining in the East beyond them far;
   And to the earth it gave great light,
   And so it continued day and night.
   (Chorus)

3. This star drew nigh to the northwest;
   O'er Bethlehem it took its rest,
   And there it did both stop and stay,
   Right o'er the place where Jesus lay.
   (Chorus)

4. Then entered in those Wise Men three,
   Full rev'rently upon their knee,
   And offered there in His presence
   Their gold and myrrh and frankincense.
   (Chorus)

Children (and most adults) love animals. In this charming 12th-century English carol, every animal in the stable has a special task: the donkey has brought Mary to Bethlehem; the cow has given up her manger for the baby Jesus; the sheep has given its wool for a blanket; the dove coos the baby to sleep; and even the stubborn, bad-tempered camel has brought the Wise Men to worship at the baby's manger.

THE FRIENDLY BEASTS

Traditional

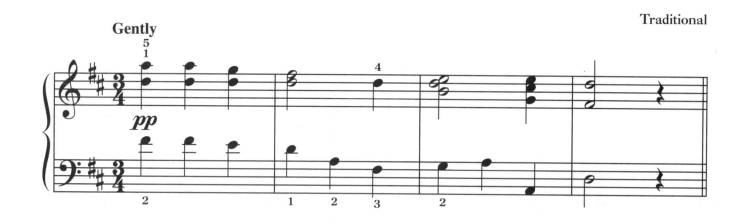

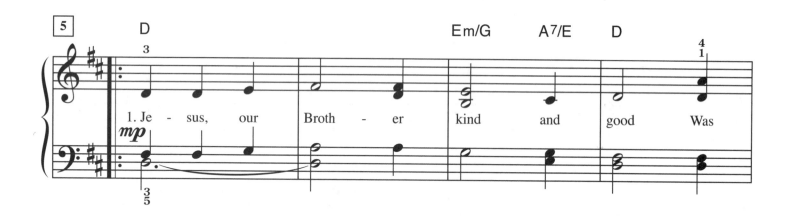

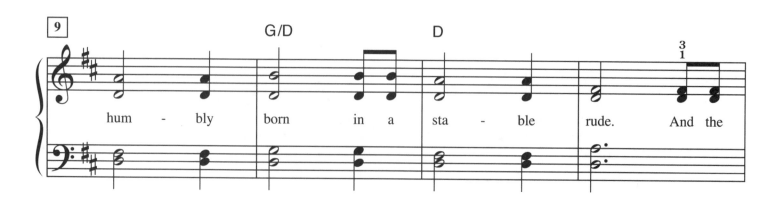

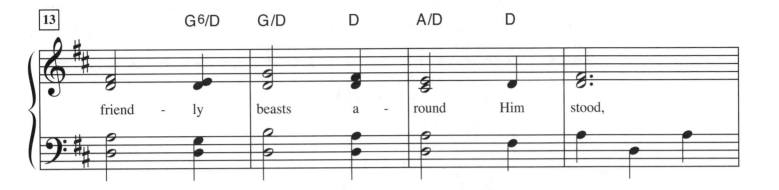

friend - ly beasts a - round Him stood,

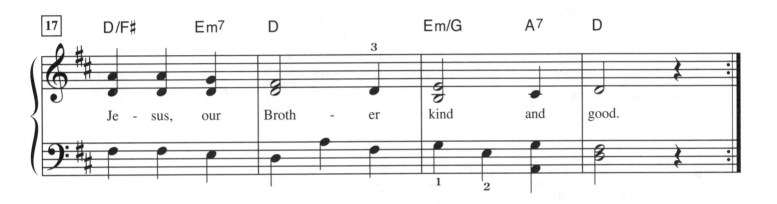

Je - sus, our Broth - er kind and good.

2. "I," said the donkey, shaggy and brown,
   "I carried His mother up hill and down;
   I carried her safely to Bethlehem town.
   I," said the donkey, shaggy and brown.

3. "I," said the cow, all white and red,
   "I gave Him my manger for a bed;
   I gave Him my hay to pillow His head.
   I," said the cow, all white and red.

4. "I," said the sheep with curly horn,
   "I gave Him my wool for His blanket warm;
   He wore my coat on Christmas morn.
   I," said the sheep with curly horn.

5. "I," said the dove from the rafters high,
   "Cooed Him to sleep that He should not cry;
   We cooed Him to sleep, my mate and I.
   I," said the dove from the rafters high.

6. "I," said the camel, yellow and black,
   "Over the desert, upon my back
   I brought Him a gift in the Wise Men's pack.
   I," said the camel, yellow and black.

7. Thus every beast by some good spell
   In the stable dark was glad to tell
   Of the gift he gave Emmanuel,
   The gift he gave Emmanuel.

Italian-born composer Pietro A. Yon (1886–1943) won many prizes for performance on piano and organ before coming to the United States in 1907. After several prestigious appointments as organist, Yon became the organist at St. Patrick's Cathedral in New York City. Among his many choral and organ works, this piece—composed in 1917—is the best known. In this work, he ingeniously combines his own melody with the traditional *Adeste Fideles*.

GESÚ BAMBINO
(THE INFANT JESUS)

Words and Music by
Pietro A. Yon

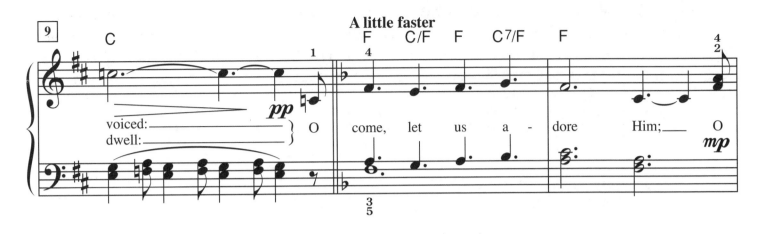

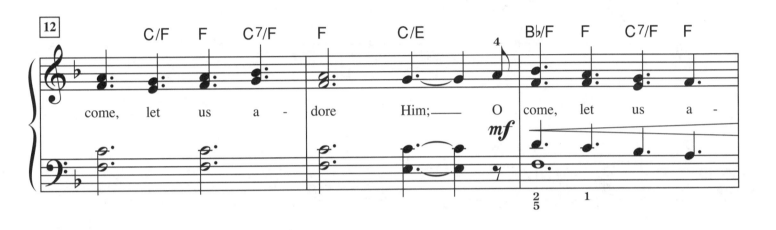

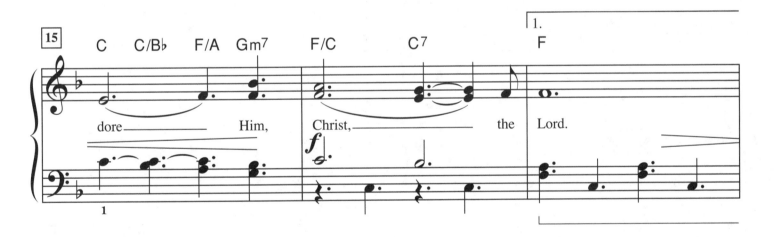

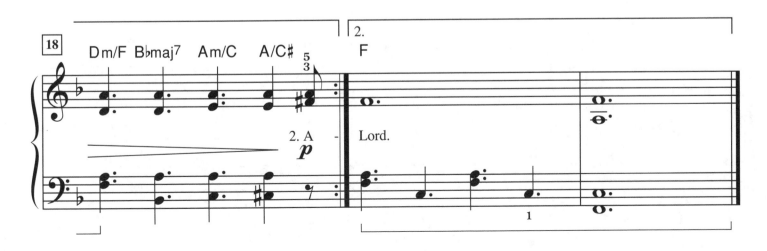

This is a very old carol. The word "ye" is an archaic form of the plural of "you." The word "rest" means "keep." Therefore, the title means "May God Keep You Merry, Gentlemen." The music is written in the medieval Aeolian mode in D (D E F G A Bb C D). The song was first published in 1827 and was well known to Charles Dickens, who mentions it in his famous book, *A Christmas Carol.*

GOD REST YE MERRY, GENTLEMEN

Traditional

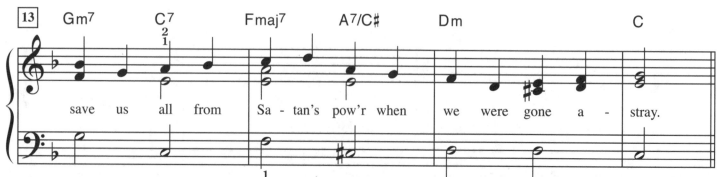

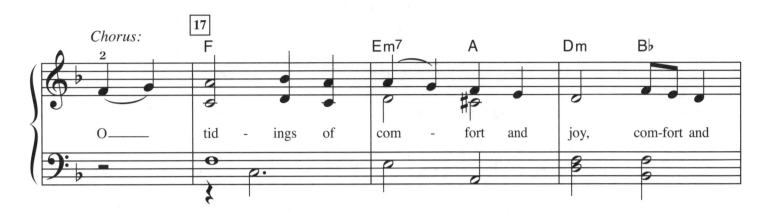

Chorus:

17 F | Em⁷ | A | Dm | B♭

O_____ tid - ings of com - fort and joy, com-fort and

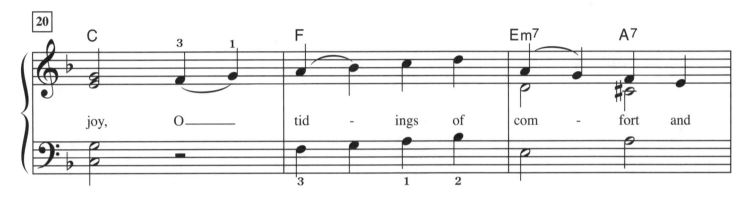

20 C | F | Em⁷ | A⁷

joy, O_____ tid - ings of com - fort and

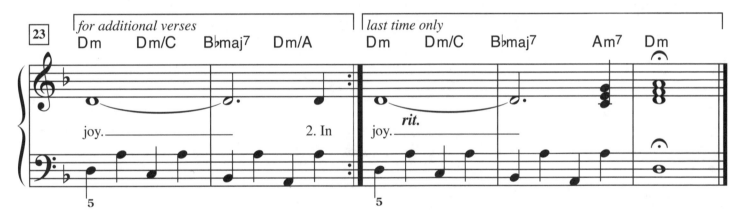

for additional verses

23 Dm | Dm/C | B♭maj⁷ | Dm/A

last time only

Dm | Dm/C | B♭maj⁷ | Am⁷ | Dm

joy._____   2. In   joy._____ *rit.*

2. In Bethlehem in Jewry this blesséd Babe was born,
   And laid within a manger upon this blesséd morn;
   To which His mother Mary did nothing take in scorn.
   (Chorus)

3. From God our heavenly Father a blesséd angel came,
   And unto certain shepherds brought tidings of the same,
   How that in Bethlehem was born the Son of God by name.
   (Chorus)

4. "Fear not," then said the angel, "Let nothing you affright;
   This day was born a Savior of a pure Virgin bright
   To free all those who trust in Him from Satan's power
   and might."
   (Chorus)

5. The shepherds at those tidings rejoicéd much in mind
   And left their flocks a-feeding in tempest, storm and wind,
   And went to Bethlehem straightaway this blesséd Babe to find.
   (Chorus)

6. But when to Bethlehem they came where at this Infant lay,
   They found Him in a manger where oxen feed on hay;
   His Mother Mary kneeling unto the Lord did pray.
   (Chorus)

7. Now to the Lord sing praises, all you within this place,
   And with true love and brotherhood each other now embrace;
   This holy tide of Christmas all others doth deface.
   (Chorus)

Wenceslas was a real king who lived in Bohemia (now part of the Czech Republic) about 1,000 years ago. He earned a reputation for kindness and generosity, but was murdered by a jealous younger brother. In 1853 an American priest, John Mason Neale, was given a collection of church and school songs, which included a 13th-century Latin song called *Tempus adest floridum* (*Spring Has Unfolded Her Flowers*). He wrote new words and published the result—the carol we know as "Good King Wenceslas."

GOOD KING WENCESLAS

Traditional

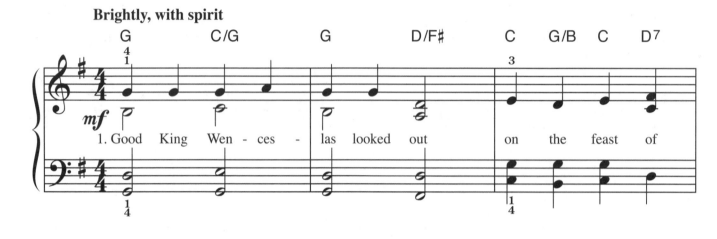

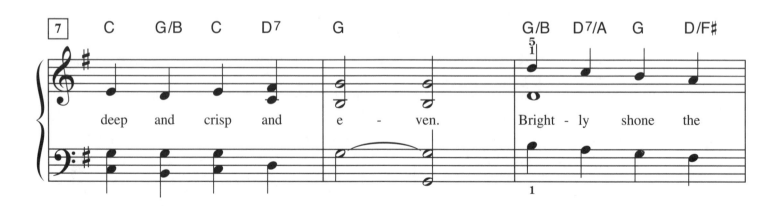

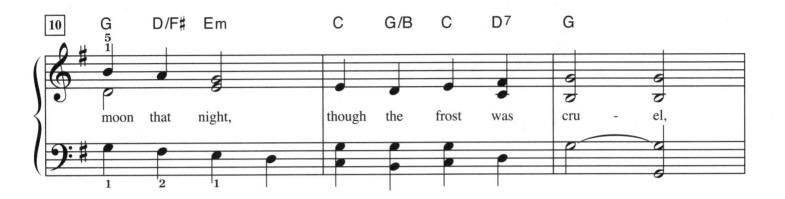

10 G | D/F♯ Em | C G/B C D7 | G

moon that night, | though the frost was | cru - el,

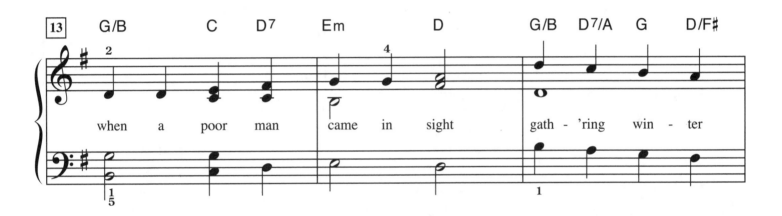

13 G/B | C D7 Em | D | G/B D7/A G D/F♯

when a poor man | came in sight | gath - 'ring win - ter

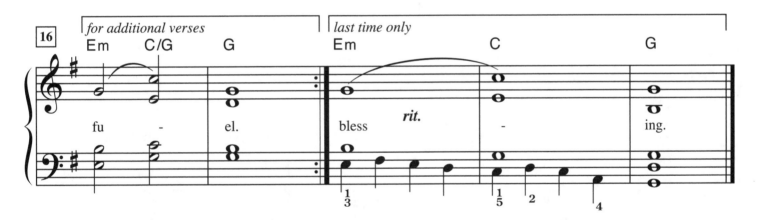

for additional verses | *last time only*

16 Em C/G G | Em | C | G

fu - el. | bless *rit.* | - | ing.

2. "Hither, page, and stand by me,
   If thou know'st it, telling,
   Yonder peasant, who is he?
   Where and what his dwelling?"
   "Sire, he lives a good league hence
   Underneath the mountain,
   Right against the forest fence,
   By Saint Agnes' fountain."

3. "Bring me flesh and bring me wine,
   Bring me pine logs hither:
   Thou and I will see him dine
   When we bear them thither."
   Page and monarch, forth they went,
   Forth they went together
   Through the rude wind's wild lament
   And the bitter weather.

4. "Sire, the night is darker now
   And the wind blows stronger;
   Fails my heart, I know not how
   I can go no longer."
   "Mark my footsteps, good my page,
   Tread thou in them boldly;
   Thou shalt find the winter's rage
   Freeze thy blood less coldly."

5. In his master's steps he trod
   Where the snow lay dinted;
   Heat was in the very sod
   Which the Saint had printed.
   Therefore, Christian men be sure
   Wealth or rank possessing,
   Ye who now will bless the poor
   Shall yourselves find blessing.

Until the Civil War, white America had pretty much ignored African-American music. However, during the war, several white officers of black regiments wrote down the melodies they heard the soldiers singing. The first collection of these songs was published in 1867. Shortly after that, an African-American choral group called the Fisk University Jubilee Singers made many of these melodies, now known as spirituals, widely known.

Go, Tell It on the Mountain

African-American Spiritual

Cledus T. Judd, the country singer who recorded this comedy song said: "A couple of good friends of mine, Elmo and Patsy, wrote me and said they's written the perfect country Christmas song. I said, 'You pretty much got it all: Grandma, the family, getting drunk and run over by heavy machinery.' "

Grandma Got Run Over by a Reindeer

Words and Music by
Randy Brooks

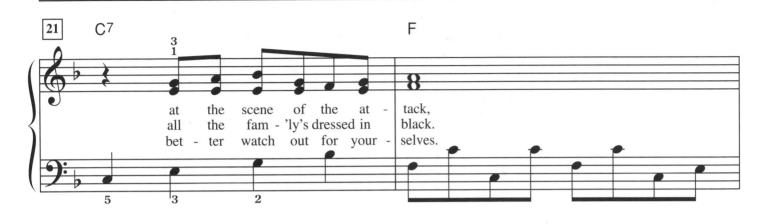

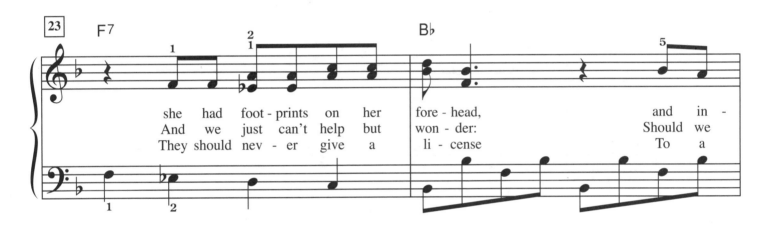

Felix Mendelssohn was only 17 when his delightful overture to Shakespeare's *A Midsummer Night's Dream* established him as a genius in the European musical world. In his short life of only 38 years, Mendelssohn went on to write a huge amount of music of every type, including an 1840 choral work that celebrated the invention of printing. Some of this music was later adapted to words by Charles Wesley, brother of the man who founded Methodism. The hymn has become a favorite in Great Britain and the United States, even though Mendelssohn himself thought it unsuitable for a sacred text.

HARK! THE HERALD ANGELS SING

Words by Charles Wesley
Music by Felix Mendelssohn

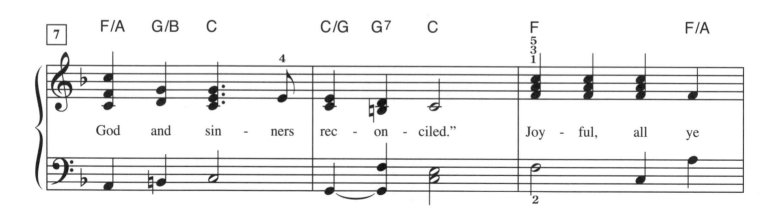

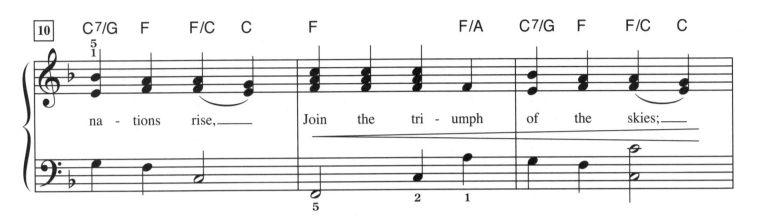

10 C7/G F F/C C F F/A C7/G F F/C C

na - tions rise,___ Join the tri - umph of the skies;___

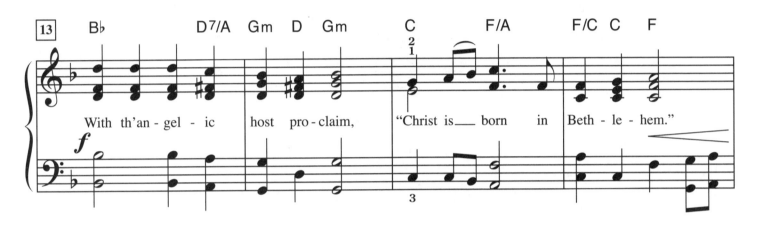

13 B♭ D7/A Gm D Gm C F/A F/C C F

With th'an - gel - ic host pro - claim, "Christ is___ born in Beth - le - hem."

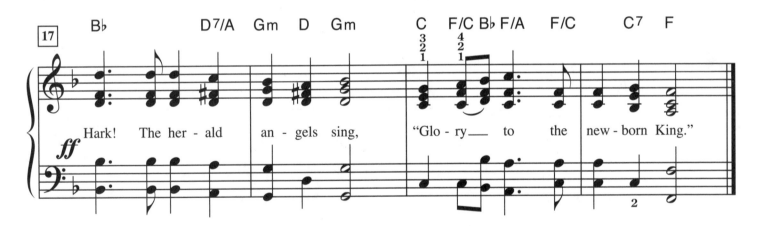

17 B♭ D7/A Gm D Gm C F/C B♭ F/A F/C C7 F

Hark! The her - ald an - gels sing, "Glo - ry___ to the new - born King."

2. Christ, by highest heav'n adored,
   Christ the everlasting Lord,
   Late in time behold Him come,
   Offspring of the Virgin's womb!
   Veiled in flesh the Godhead see;
   Hail th'incarnate Deity!
   Pleased as Man with men to dwell,
   Jesus, our Immanuel,
   Hark! The herald angels sing,
   "Glory to the newborn King."

3. Hail the heav'n-born Prince of Peace!
   Hail the Sun of Righteousness!
   Light and life to all He brings,
   Ris'n with healing in His wings.
   Mild He lays His glory by,
   Born that man no more may die,
   Born to raise the sons of earth,
   Born to give them second birth.
   Hark! The herald angels sing,
   "Glory to the newborn King."

The 1944 Hollywood movie *Meet Me in St. Louis* tells the story of an average American family that goes to the 1904 World's Fair. The score is full of great songs, including "The Trolley Song," "The Boy Next Door," and this one, "Have Yourself a Merry Little Christmas," all sung by the immortal Judy Garland.

HAVE YOURSELF A MERRY LITTLE CHRISTMAS

Words and Music by
Hugh Martin and Ralph Blane

Many years ago in England, bands of roving musicians (called "waits") roved the streets during the holiday season, singing and playing in the hopes of earning a pudding, a drink, or a few pennies. This song, also called "The Wassail Song," was a popular waits carol of the time. "Wassail" was a drink made with ale or wine spiced with roasted apples and sugar. The word comes from an old Anglo-Saxon toast, "waes hael," which means "be healthy."

HERE WE COME A-CAROLING
(THE WASSAIL SONG)

Traditional

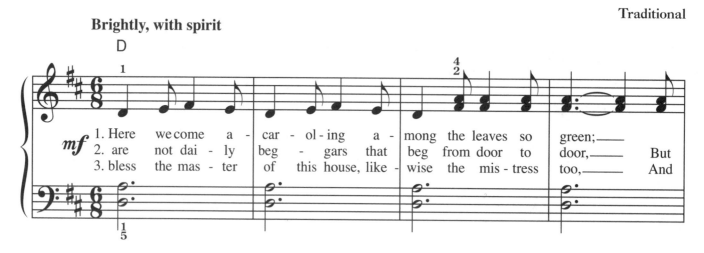

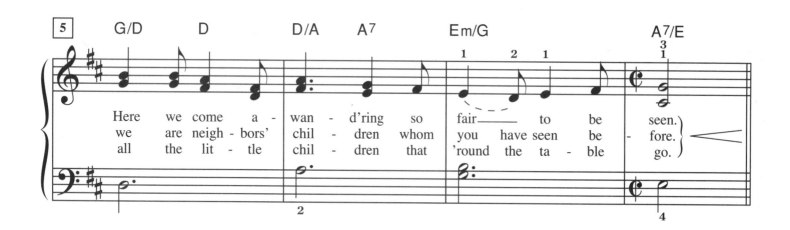

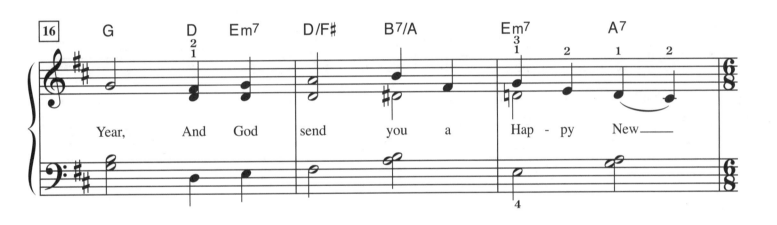

After the phenomenal success of "Rudolph the Red-Nosed Reindeer" in 1949, songwriter Johnny Marks started his own publishing company, named it "St. Nicholas Music," and started turning out more Christmas songs. This song dates from 1964 and was sung by Burl Ives on a television Christmas special.

A Holly Jolly Christmas

Words and Music by
Johnny Marks

If you've ever been away from home when Christmas rolls around, you'll understand why this song remains popular after more than 50 years. The lyrics call to mind the many joys of spending the holidays with friends and family.

(THERE'S NO PLACE LIKE)
HOME FOR THE HOLIDAYS

Words by Al Stillman
Music by Robert Allen

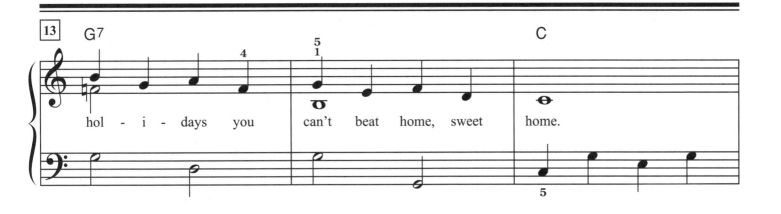

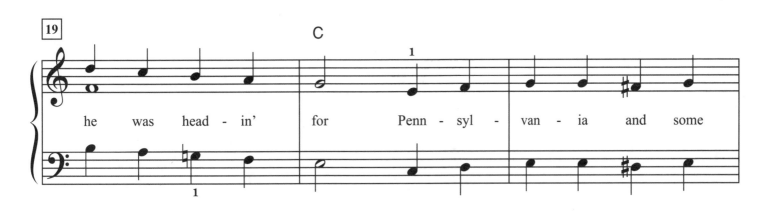

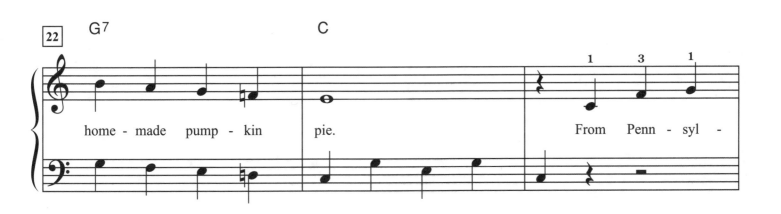

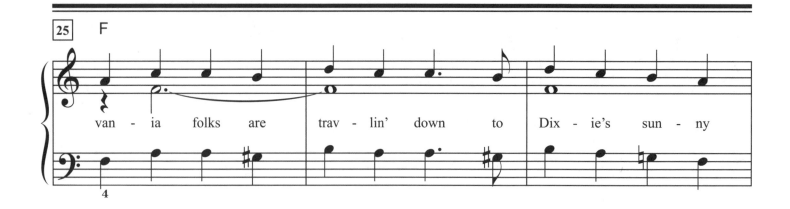

van - ia folks are trav - lin' down to Dix - ie's sun - ny

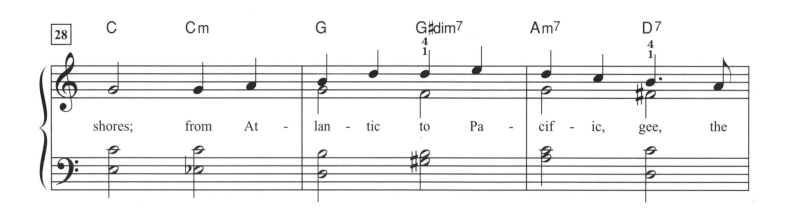

shores; from At - lan - tic to Pa - cif - ic, gee, the

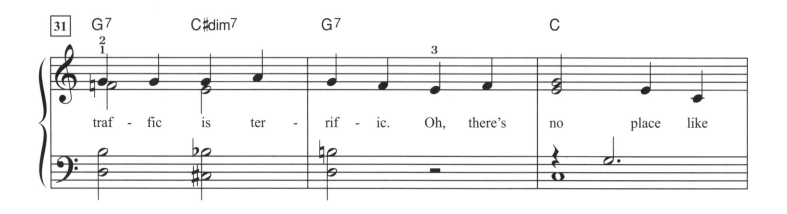

traf - fic is ter - rif - ic. Oh, there's no place like

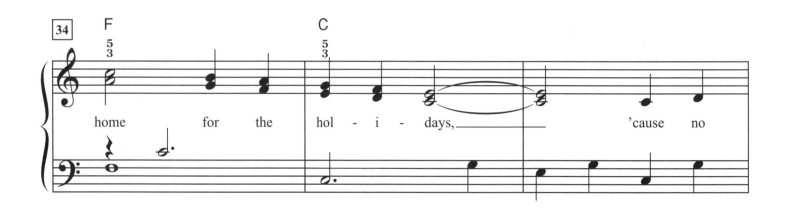

home for the hol - i - days,_____ 'cause no

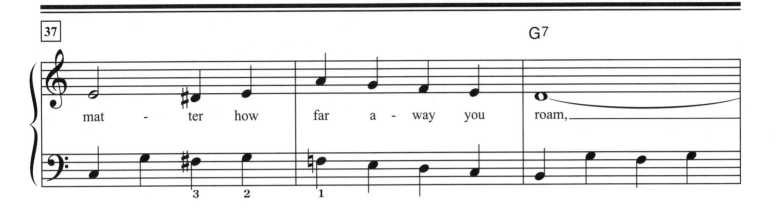

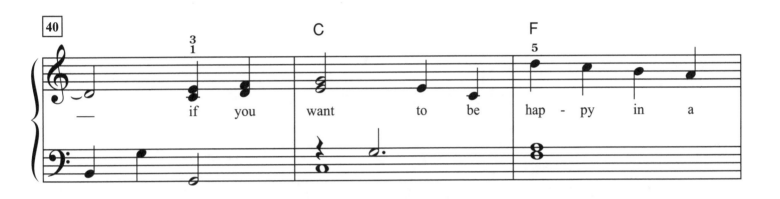

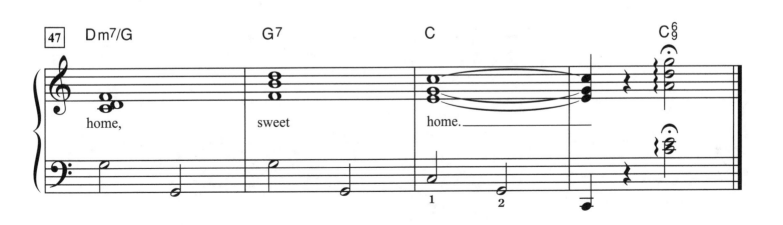

Since young Adolphe Charles Adam wanted to be a composer—against his father's wishes—Adolphe studied music in secret. When his father found out, he recognized the boy's talent and relented on the condition that he never write for the stage. After Adolphe had become France's most famous composer of comic operas, his father finally forgave him. Today, Adolphe Charles Adam is chiefly remembered for his charming ballet *Giselle*, and *Cantique de Noël*, which we call "O Holy Night." The English words were written by Boston music critic and teacher John Sullivan Dwight (1818–1893).

O Holy Night
(CANTIQUE DE NOËL)

Words by Placide Cappeau
English translation by John Sullivan Dwight
Music by Adolphe Charles Adam

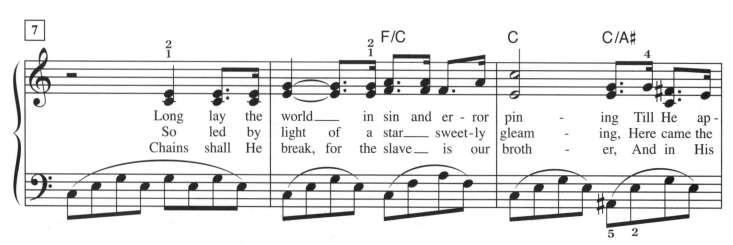

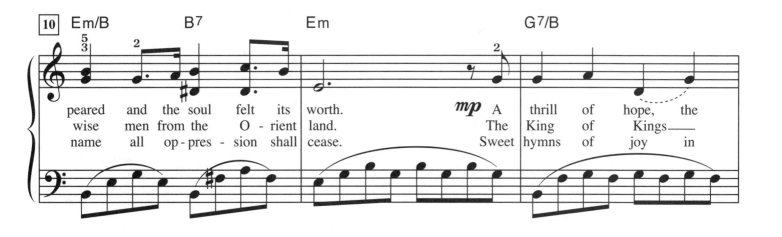

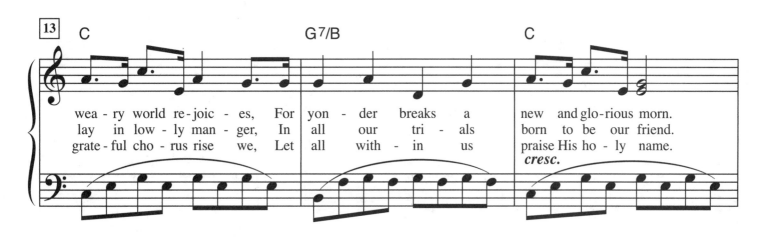

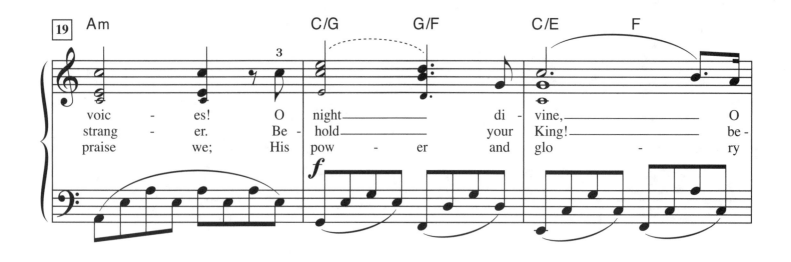

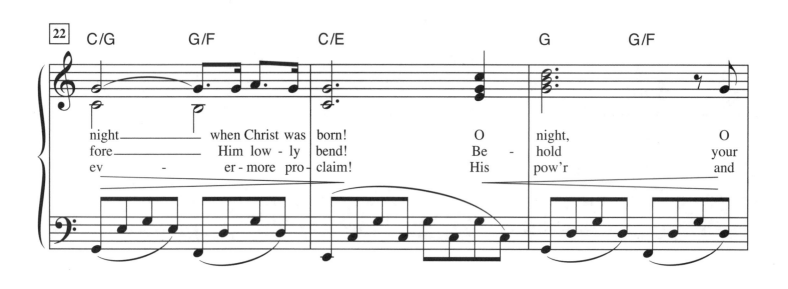

In the 19th century, Henry Wadsworth Longfellow (1807–1882) was one of America's favorite poets. His many works include *Song of Hiawatha* and a translation of Dante's *Divine Comedy*. The words to this powerful statement of faith were set to music by British pianist, organist, and composer Jean Baptiste Calkin (1827–1905). In modern times, the same words were set to music by Johnny Marks (of "Rudolph, the Red-Nosed Reindeer" fame).

I Heard the Bells on Christmas Day

Words by Henry Wadsworth Longfellow
Music by Jean Baptiste Calkin

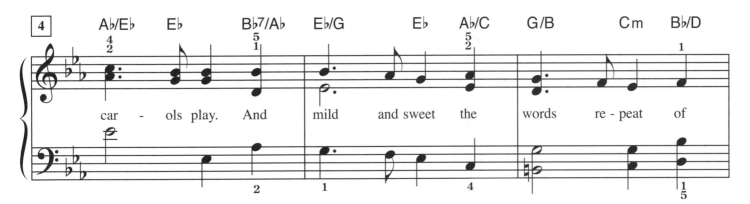

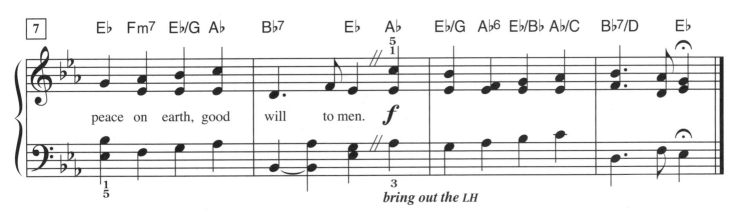

2. I thought how, as the day had come,
   The belfries of all Christendom
   Had rolled along th'unbroken song
   Of peace on earth, good will to men.

3. And in despair I bow'd my head:
   "There is no peace on earth," I said,
   "For hate is strong, and mocks the song
   Of peace on earth, good will to men."

4. Then pealed the bells more loud and deep:
   "God is not dead, nor doth He sleep;
   The wrong shall fail, the right prevail,
   With peace on earth, good will to men."

5. Till, ringing, singing on its way,
   The world revolved from night to day,
   A voice, a chime, a chant sublime,
   Of peace on earth, good will to men!

It seems that songs that become popular during the stress of wartime come to have a more profound meaning. Such is the case with this lovely ballad, made popular by Bing Crosby's heartfelt rendition, recorded during World War II. The last two lines of the song had special meaning to many American GIs.

I'll Be Home for Christmas

Lyrics by Kim Gannon
Music by Walter Kent

Unitarian minister Edmund Hamilton Sears wrote the deeply felt words of this hymn in 1849. Sears had a vision of an era of world peace that could only be attained through the coming of Christ. This hymn is often sung to a tune by Arthur Sullivan (of Gilbert and Sullivan fame), but the melody more familiar to Americans is this one, penned by Boston-born composer Richard S. Willis (1819–1900).

IT CAME UPON THE MIDNIGHT CLEAR

Words by Edmund Hamilton Sears
Music by Richard S. Willis

1. It came up-on the mid-night clear, That glo-ri-ous song of old, From an-gels bend-ing near the earth To

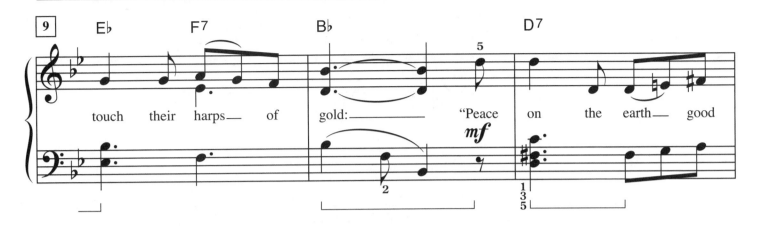

touch their harps— of gold: "Peace on the earth— good

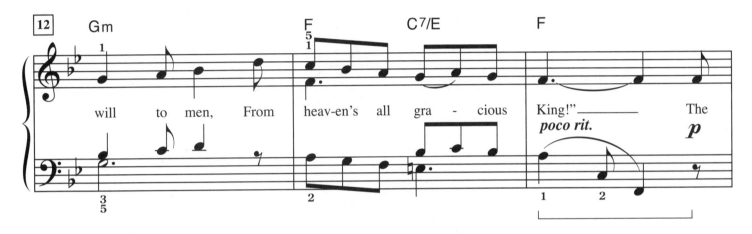

will to men, From heav-en's all gra - cious King!"———— The

world in sol - emn still - ness lay To hear the an - gels sing.————

2. Still through the cloven skies they come with peaceful wings unfurled,
   And still their heavenly music floats o'er all the weary world:
   Above its sad and lowly plains they bend on hovering wing,
   And ever o'er its Babel sounds the blessed angels sing.

3. Yet with the woes of sin and strife the world has suffered long;
   Beneath the heavenly strain have rolled two thousand years of wrong;
   And man, at war with man, hears not the tidings which they bring;
   O hush the noise, ye men of strife and hear the angels sing.

4. O ye, beneath life's crushing load, whose forms are bending low
   Who toil along the climbing way with painful steps and slow.
   Look now! for glad and golden hours come swiftly on the wing;
   O rest beside the weary road and hear the angels sing!

5. For lo! the days are hastening on, by prophet bards foretold,
   When with the ever-circling years comes round the age of gold;
   When peace shall over all the earth its ancient splendors fling,
   And the whole world send back the song which now the angels sing.

The Bible makes no mention of either the Virgin Mary or the Baby Jesus ever having set foot on a ship. And, of course, Bethlehem is nowhere near the sea. Nevertheless, this carol depicting Mary and Jesus on a ship has been sung for over 300 years, and is as popular as ever.

I Saw Three Ships

Traditional

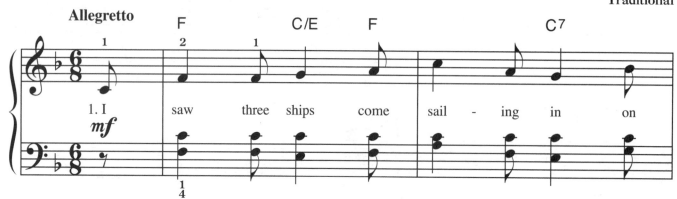

2. And what was in those ships all three,
   On Christmas Day, on Christmas Day?
   And what was in those ships all three,
   On Christmas Day in the morning?

3. Our Savior Christ and His Lady...
   (continue similarly)

4. Pray, whither sailed those ships all three?...

5. O, they sailed into Bethlehem...

6. And all the bells on earth shall ring...

7. And all the angels in Heav'n shall sing...

8. And all the souls on earth shall sing...

9. Then let us all rejoice amain...

Who can argue with the sentiments expressed in this happy Christmas waltz? Kids and jingle bells, friends coming to call, parties and caroling... even the scary ghost stories (no doubt a reference to Charles Dickens' *A Christmas Carol*) leave everyone happy. Songwriters Eddie Pola and George Wylie penned this upbeat tune in 1963.

It's the Most Wonderful Time of the Year

Words and Music by
Eddie Pola and George Wylie

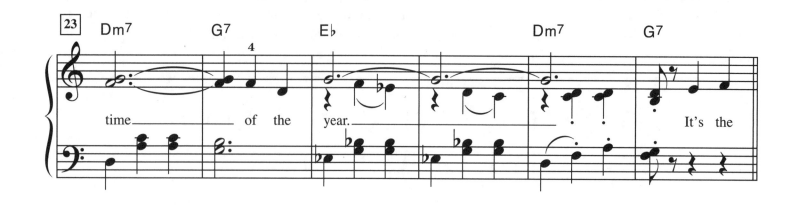

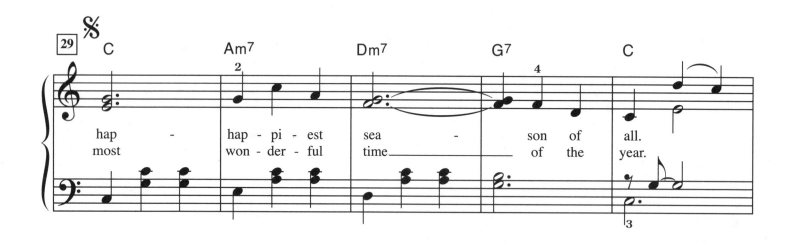

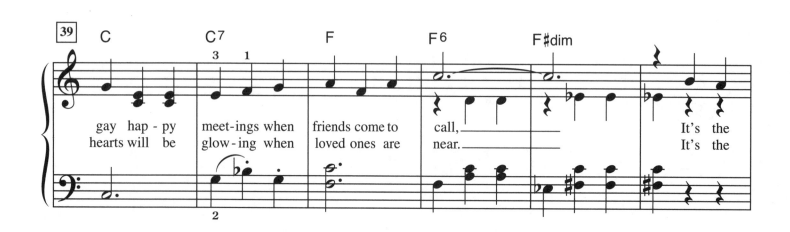

Although he came from a famous, wealthy family, James Pierpont was something of a rebel. Much to the horror of his abolitionist father, he espoused the Confederate cause before the Civil War, and even moved to the South. Pierpont wrote many songs, but is remembered only for this one. The song was actually written for Thanksgiving under the title "The One-Horse Open Sleigh," but the Christmas-like jingle bell rhythm of the chorus proved irresistible, and the song went on to become the best-known Christmas song in the world.

JINGLE BELLS

Words and Music by
James Pierpont

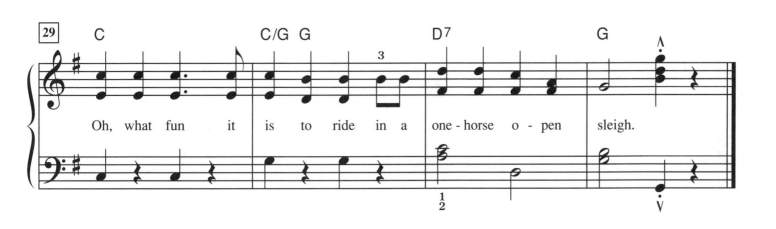

Back in the mid-50s, rock and roll was starting to dominate record sales and airplay… so it's no wonder that the Christmas season would soon be "invaded" as well. Amateur songwriters Joe Beal and Jim Boothe hit it big with this Christmas song in a best-selling record by Bobby Helms, which is still played every Christmas a half century later!

JINGLE BELL ROCK

Words and Music by
Joe Beal and Jim Boothe

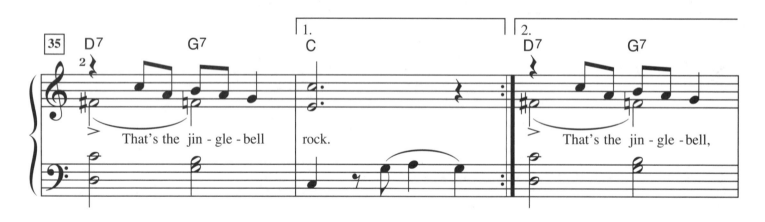

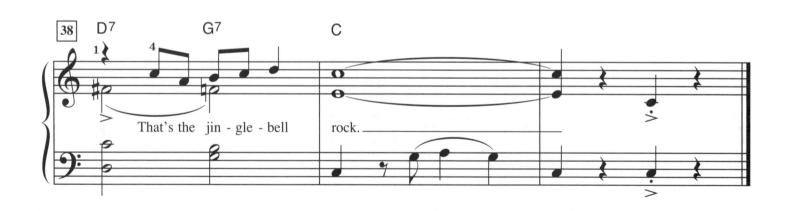

The original St. Nicholas was a 4th-century bishop in Asia Minor (present-day Turkey), who was credited with having miraculous powers. During a famine, he promised sailors that if they gave their ships' cargo of grain to feed the townspeople, they would find their ships miraculously refilled. Sure enough, the miracle was fulfilled and the sailors became his first converts. Nicholas eventually became the patron saint of many countries, including the Netherlands. The Dutch brought traditions associated with St. Nicholas to the New World, especially to New York City, which was a Dutch colony until 1664. It was here in the New World that St. Nicholas became known as Santa Claus.

Jolly Old St. Nicholas

Traditional

When young Isaac Watts complained to his minister father that the hymns they sang in church were of inferior quality, his father challenged him to write better ones. By the following Sunday, Isaac had turned out the first of hundreds of beautiful lyrics that he would write during his lifetime. *Joy to the World* comes from his 1719 collection *The Psalms of David, Imitated*. Fully 120 years later, American music teacher Lowell Mason set the words to music. Because he used themes from *Messiah*, Mason modestly gave credit to his idol, composer George Frideric Handel.

JOY TO THE WORLD

Words by Isaac Watts
Music by Lowell Mason
(after George Frideric Handel)

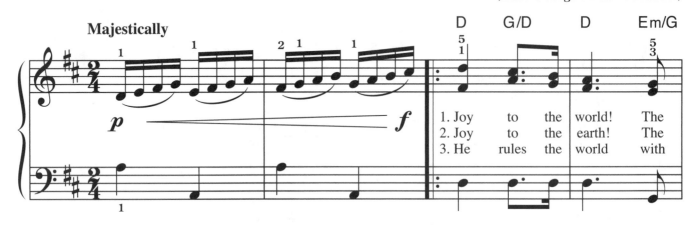

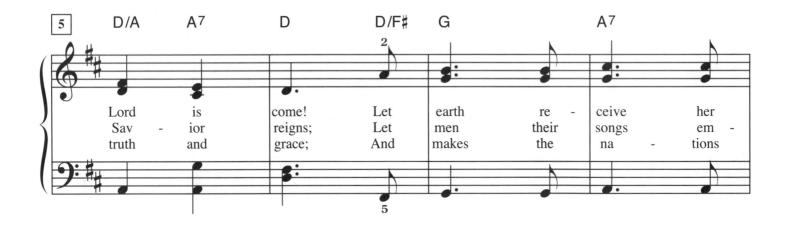

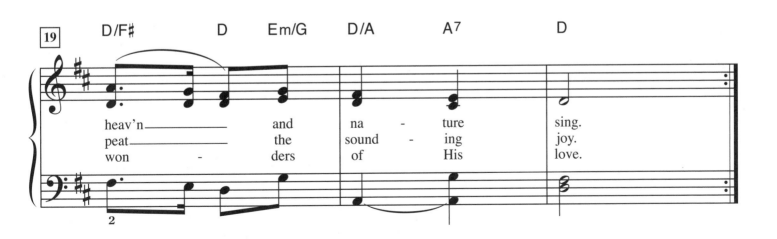

The famous songwriting team of Sammy Cahn and Jule Styne had one of their biggest hits with this Christmas song from 1945. When someone told Cahn that they thought "let it snow" was a common English expression and therefore couldn't be copyrighted, he replied, "Maybe once, maybe twice, but say it three times—and it's mine!"

Let It Snow! Let It Snow! Let It Snow!

Words by Sammy Cahn
Music by Jule Styne

In this charming fable, a poor little drummer boy gives the Baby Jesus the only gift he can afford: a song on his drum. His gift is as appreciated as the rich gifts the Wise Men bring (not a bad lesson to remember in this day of seasonal overspending). Harry Simeone, one of the writers, made the song a hit in 1958 with his choral group.

THE LITTLE DRUMMER BOY

Words and Music by
Katherine Davis, Henry Onorati
and Harry Simeone

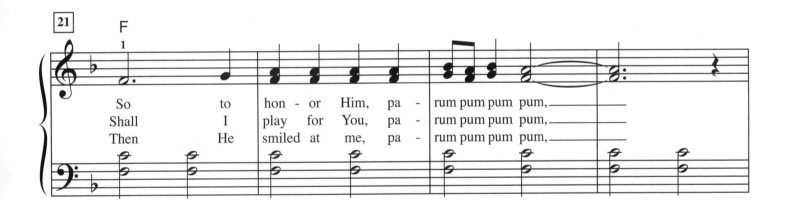

In December of 1865, Phillips Brooks, a 30-year-old minister from Philadelphia, was in the Holy Land. On Christmas Eve, he traveled on horseback to Bethlehem to visit the site where the shepherds had been when they saw the Star. Brooks was deeply moved by the experience and later wrote the words for *O Little Town of Bethlehem*, intending it as a children's hymn. He gave his poem to his church's organist, Lewis Redner, who composed the lovely melody in time for Christmas 1868.

O LITTLE TOWN OF BETHLEHEM

Words by Phillips Brooks
Music by Lewis H. Redner

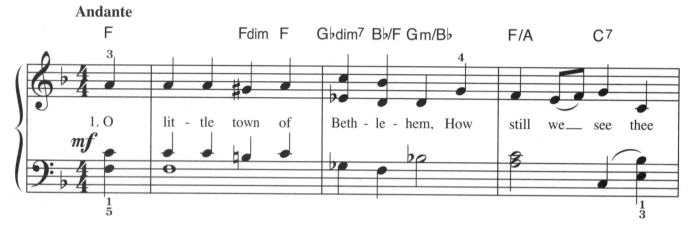

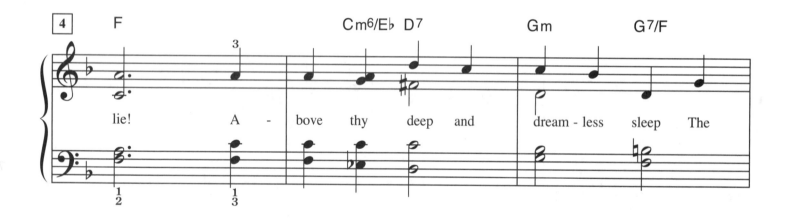

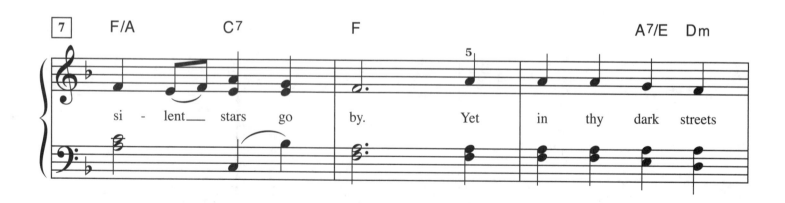

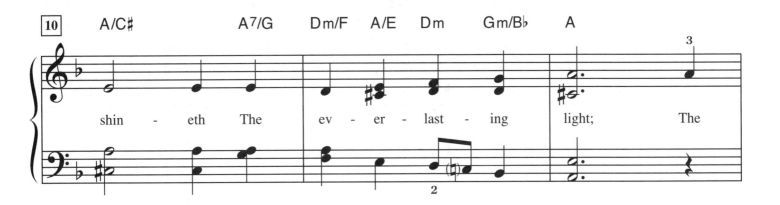

2. For Christ is born of Mary, and gathered all above,
   While mortals sleep, the angels keep their watch of wond'ring love.
   O morning stars together proclaim the holy birth!
   And praises sing to God the King and peace to men on earth.

3. How silently, how silently the wond'rous gift is giv'n!
   So God imparts to human hearts the blessings of His heav'n.
   No ear may hear His coming, but in this world of sin,
   Where meek souls will receive Him still, the dear Christ enters in.

4. Where children pure and happy pray to the blessed Child,
   Where misery cries out to Thee, Son of the mother mild;
   Where charity stands watching and faith holds wide the door,
   The dark night wakes, the glory breaks, and Christmas comes once more.

5. O holy Child of Bethlehem, descend to us we pray;
   Cast out our sin and enter in, be born in us today.
   We hear the Christmas angels the great glad tidings tell;
   O come to us, abide with us, our Lord, Immanuel.

Hundreds of years before the birth of Jesus, the rose was associated with Aphrodite, the Greek goddess of love. According to legend, a bee stung Aphrodite's son Cupid when he stopped to smell a rose. Enraged, he shot an arrow into the bush, which is how the rose acquired its thorns. During the Middle Ages, many Christian cults that worshipped the Virgin Mary sprang up. Some cults assigned her the attributes of the rose, symbolic of perfect love. In this serene German carol from 1599, Mary is the rose and Jesus is her blossom.

LO, HOW A ROSE E'ER BLOOMING

Words: 15th-century German Carol
Music by Michael Praetorius

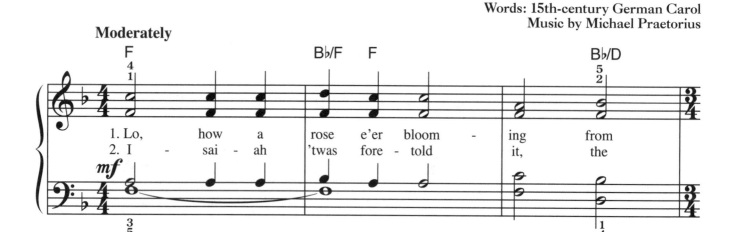

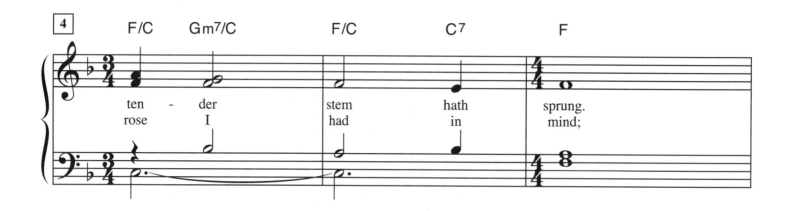

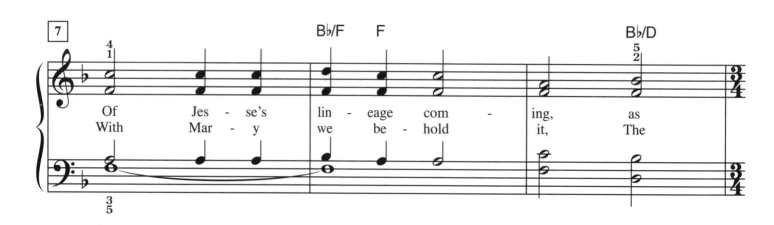

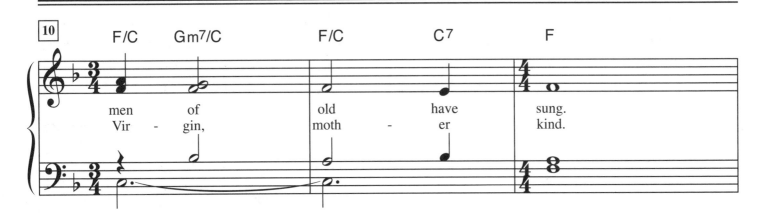

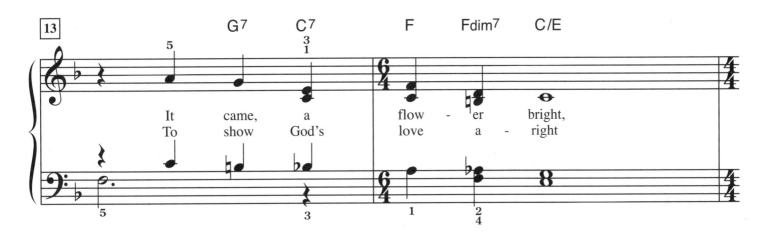

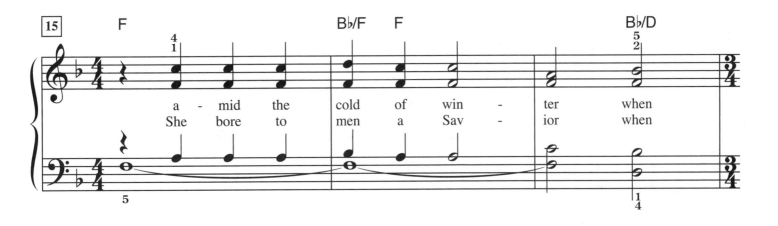

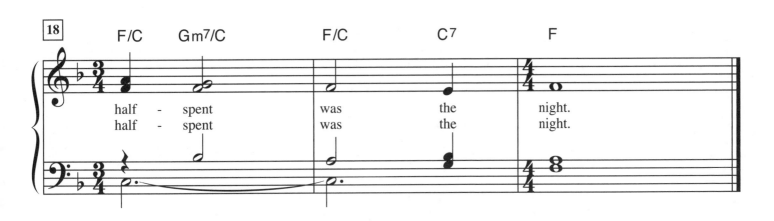

Bing Crosby had the hit on this Christmas confection back in 1949. The song was written by music business professionals Carl Sigman and Peter De Rose.

A Marshmallow World

Words by Carl Sigman
Music by Peter De Rose

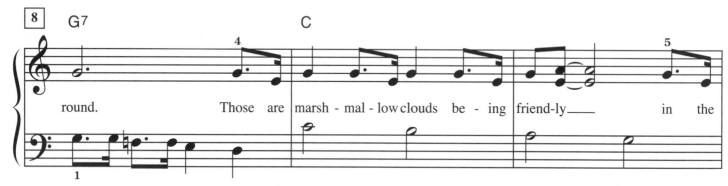

The polka is based on a peasant dance that originated in Bohemia (now the Czech Republic) in the 1830s. The name comes from the Czech word pulka (half), which refers to the characteristic short steps of the dance. The polka's popularity spread all over the world, especially to parts of the U.S. that house people of Central European origin. The Andrews Sisters' 1939 smash hit recording of "Beer Barrel Polka" (based on a Czech polka) ensured its continuing popularity in America. Burke and Webster wrote this Christmas polka in 1949.

THE MERRY CHRISTMAS POLKA

Words and Music by
Sonny Burke and Paul Webster

dance The Mer - ry Christ-mas Pol - ka;_____ Let ev - 'ry -
dance The Mer - ry Christ-mas Pol - ka;_____ Let ev - 'ry

one be hap - py and gay._____ Oh, it's the
la - dy step with her beau._____ A - round a

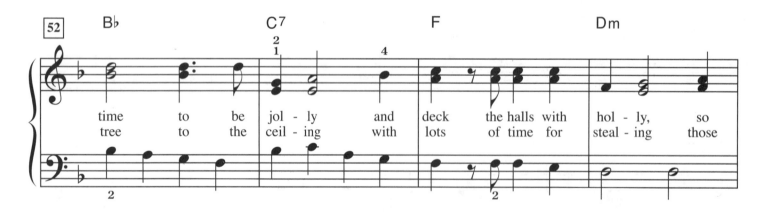

time to be jol - ly and deck the halls with hol - ly, so
tree to be the ceil - ing with lots of time for steal - ing those

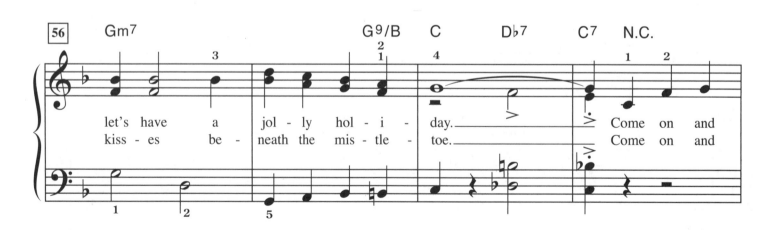

let's have a jol - ly hol - i - day._____ Come on and
kiss - es be - neath the mis - tle - toe._____ Come on and

dance _____ The Mer - ry Christ-mas Pol - ka; _____ an - oth - er
dance _____ The Mer - ry Christ-mas Pol - ka; _____ with ev - 'ry -

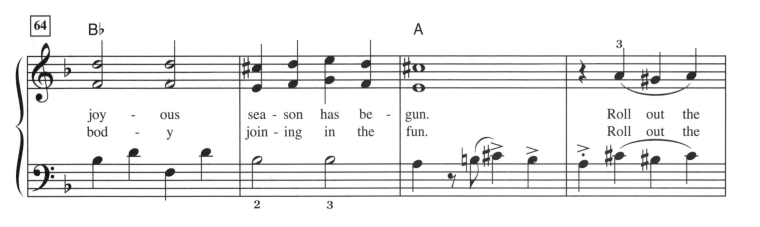

joy - ous season has be - gun. Roll out the
bod - y join - ing in the fun. Roll out the

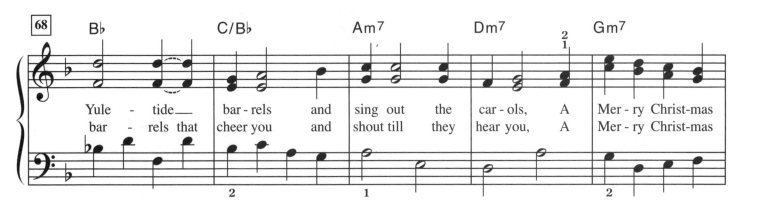

Yule - tide _____ bar - rels and sing out the car - ols, A Mer - ry Christ-mas
bar - rels that cheer you and shout till they hear you, A Mer - ry Christ-mas

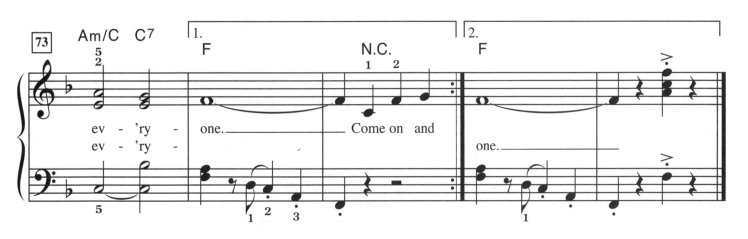

ev - 'ry - one. _____ Come on and
ev - 'ry - one. _____

Although many people knew how to say "Merry Christmas" in other languages, not many knew how to say it in Hawaiian; so Hawaiian businessman R. Alex Anderson decided to write this song. Bing Crosby liked this piece so much that he recorded it for the flip side of his biggest hit, "White Christmas."

MELE KALIKIMAKA

Words and Music by R. Alex Anderson

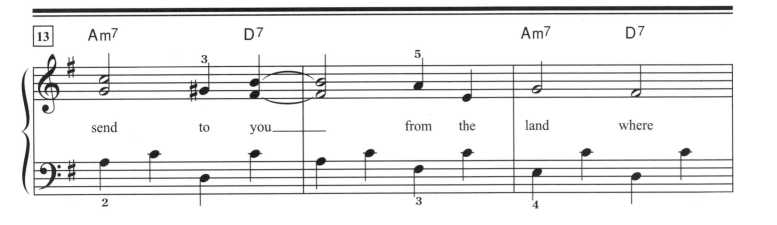

send   to   you____   from   the   land   where

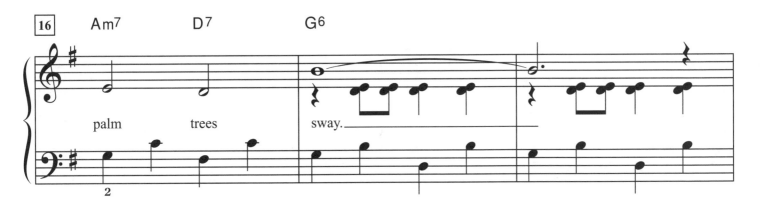

palm   trees   sway.____

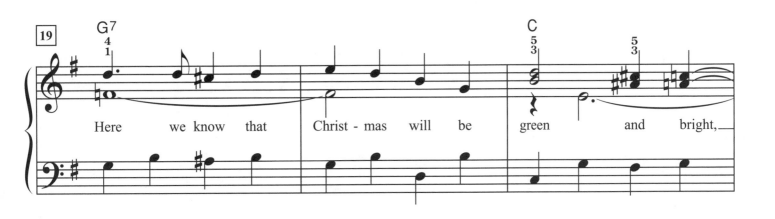

Here   we know   that   Christ - mas   will   be   green   and   bright,____

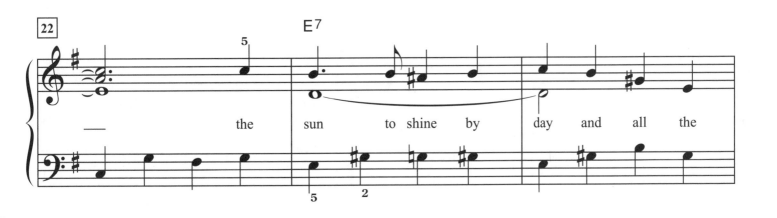

____   the   sun   to   shine   by   day   and   all   the

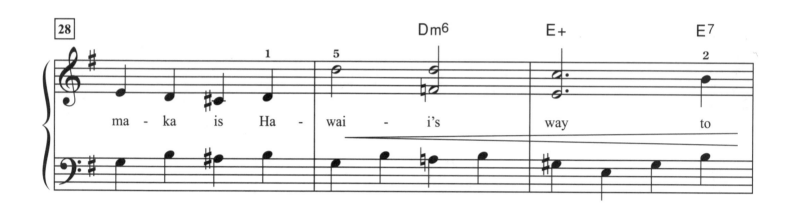

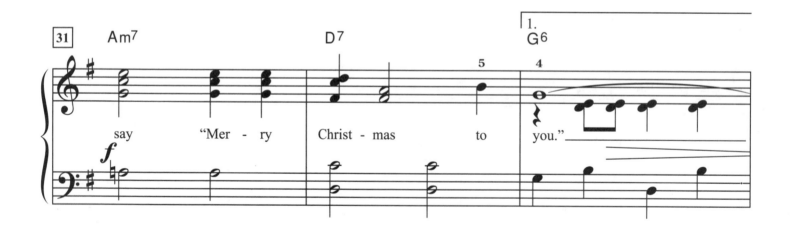

Songwriters love "laundry list" tunes—songs that enumerate a series of related things. One of writer Roy Bennett's daughters once spilled some ink on her mother's rug, and was threatened with getting "nuttin'" for Christmas. This served as the inspiration for these lyrics—a "laundry list" of naughty things a child might do—and a hit song was born.

Nuttin' for Christmas

Words and Music by
Sid Tepper and Roy C. Bennett

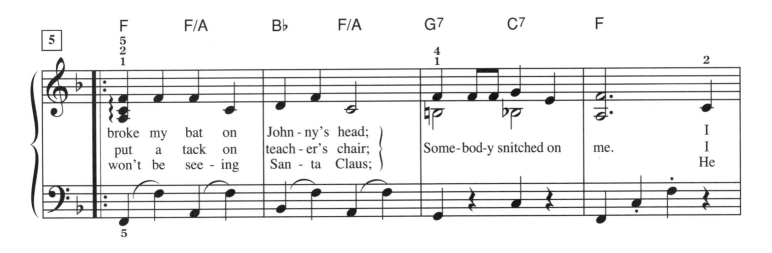

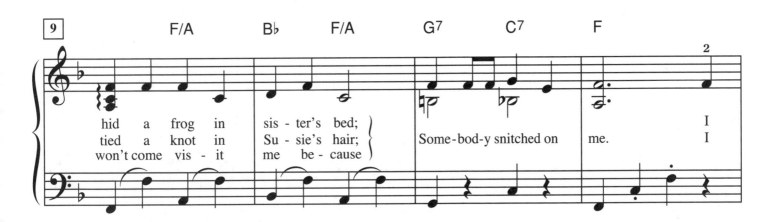

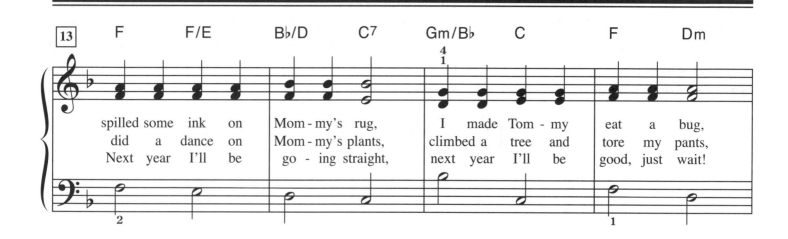

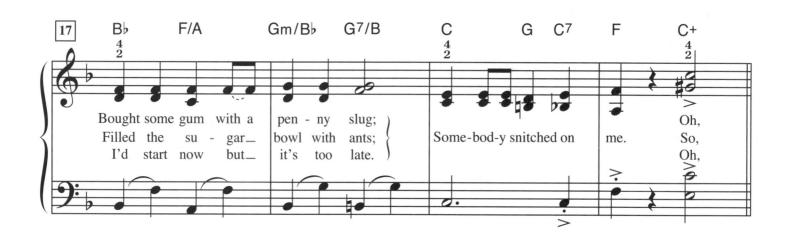

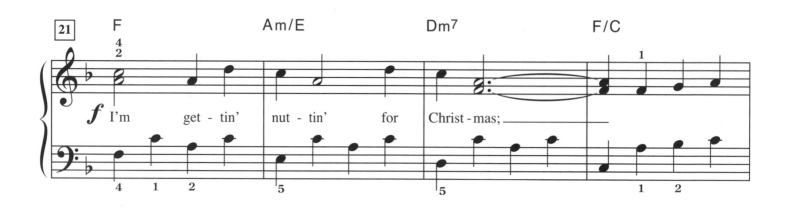

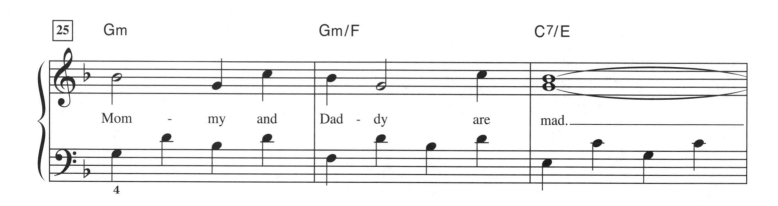

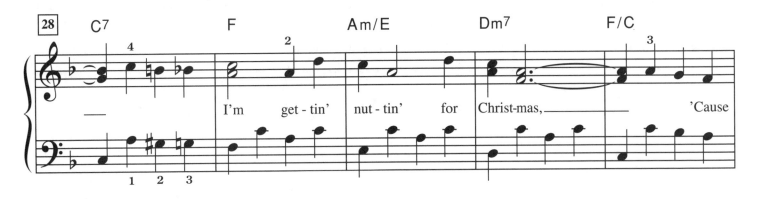

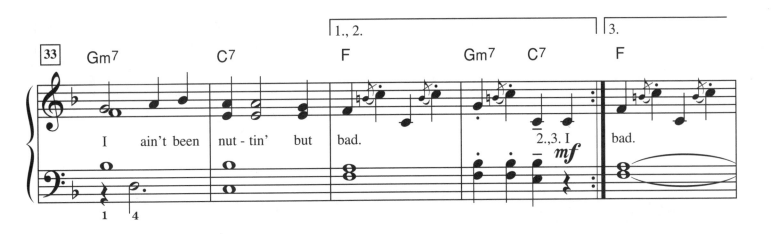

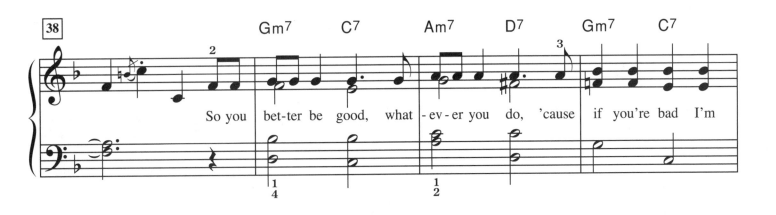

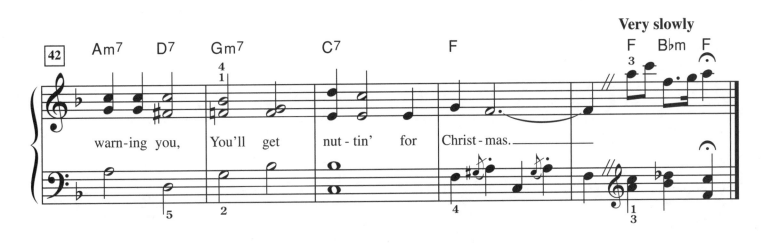

"Call-and-response" is a common pattern in African-American church music. In this spiritual, the lead singer sings "There's a star in the East on Christmas morn," and the choir answers "Rise up, shepherd, and follow." The call-and-response pattern entered the world of jazz in the 1920s through the arrangements of Fletcher Henderson and others.

RISE UP, SHEPHERD, AND FOLLOW

African-American Spiritual

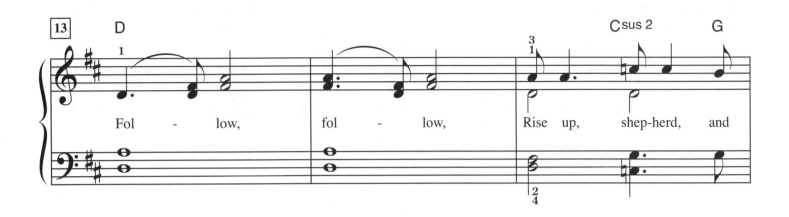

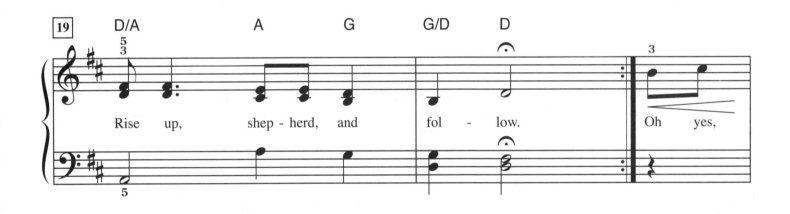

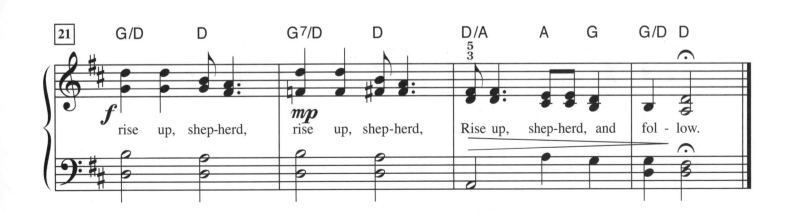

Rock and roll was in its first bloom as a new type of American music when songwriter Johnny Marks (who already had phenomenal success with "Rudolph the Red-Nosed Reindeer") contributed this effort from his prolific pen in 1958. Songstress Brenda Lee made the tune famous with her successful recording of the song.

Rockin' Around the Christmas Tree

Words and Music by
Johnny Marks

The story of "Rudolph, the Red-Nosed Reindeer" was written in 1939 by Robert L. May, as a promotional piece for the Montgomery Ward department stores. May's brother-in-law, songwriter Johnny Marks, adapted the story into a song and persuaded Gene Autry to record it. Subsequently, the song has been recorded by over 500 different artists, and went on to sell almost 200 million records and 5 million copies of sheet music, making it one of the best-selling songs of all time.

RUDOLPH, THE RED-NOSED REINDEER

Words and Music by
Johnny Marks

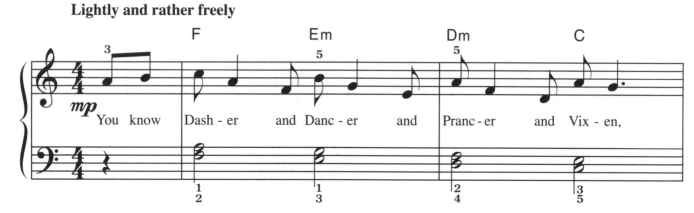

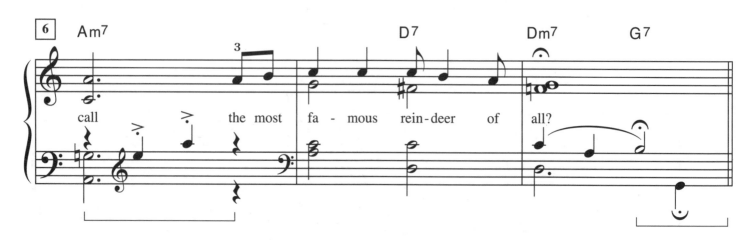

Chorus

Steady beat

Ru-dolph, the Red-Nosed Rein - deer had a ver-y shin - y nose,

And if you ev - er saw it you would e-ven say it glows.

All of the oth - er rein - deer used to laugh and call him names;

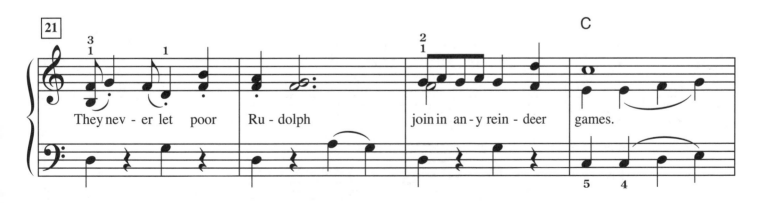

They nev - er let poor Ru - dolph join in an-y rein - deer games.

Just before Christmas in 1818, an Austrian village priest named Father Joseph Mohr noticed that the church organ had been damaged by mice and was unplayable. Needing something to sing on Christmas Eve, he dashed off some words and gave them to his organist, Franz Gruber, asking him to compose a melody that could be accompanied by a few simple guitar chords. From its first performance on that Christmas Eve till today, the quiet beauty of *Silent Night* has brought joy to millions of people.

Silent Night

Words by Joseph Mohr
Music by Franz Gruber

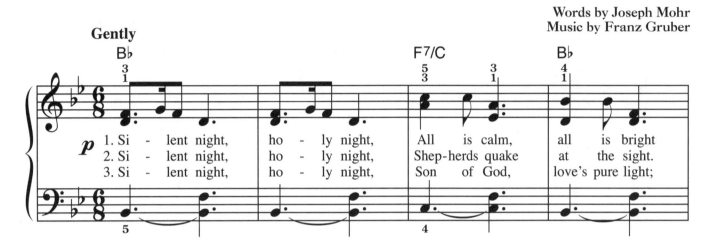

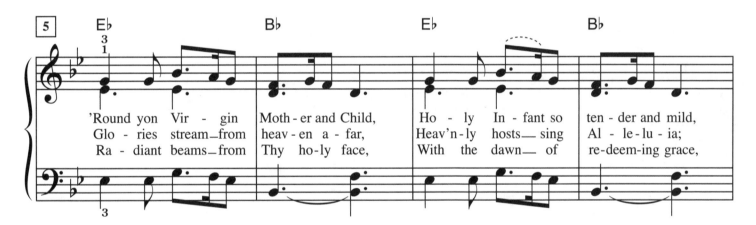

Original German words:

Stille nacht, heilige nacht!
Alles schlaft, einsam wacht
Nur das traute, hochheilige Paar,

Holder Knabe im lockigen Haar,
Schlaf in himmlischer Ruh'
Schlaf in himmlischer Ruh'.

In 1932, songwriters Haven Gillespie and J. Fred Coots came up with the idea of a song that told about a Santa Claus who rewarded good children but passed the naughty ones by. Not a single publisher was interested, but the writers finally persuaded Eddie Cantor to perform the song on his radio show. It became an instant hit and was later recorded by virtually every famous singer of the time.

Santa Claus Is Comin' To Town

Words by Haven Gillespie
Music by J. Fred Coots

A product of long-time collaborators Sid Tepper and Roy Bennett, this delightful children's song was dedicated to Tepper's daughter Susan. The title was also used in an animated Christmas cartoon, and for a doll that sold in the 1950s.

Suzy Snowflake

Words and Music by
Sid Tepper and Roy C. Bennett

Leroy Anderson (1908–1975) was one of the finest American composers of light music in the 1900s. His best-known works include "The Syncopated Clock," "Blue Tango," "Serenata," and this spirited composition, an evocation of a New England sleigh ride. Anderson was from Massachusetts, where he studied with the great composer and educator Walter Piston, among others. The song's lyricist, Mitchell Parish, wrote many lyrics for Anderson, as well as dozens of other hits including Hoagy Carmichael's "Star Dust."

SLEIGH RIDE

Words by Mitchell Parish
Music by Leroy Anderson

The 12 days last from Christmas Day to Epiphany on January 6. The custom of gift-giving arose from the first Epiphany, when the Wise Men brought gifts to the infant Jesus. This is a "cumulative" carol, with each verse mentioning an additional gift for each of the 12 days. Although this carol wasn't published until 1868, it was known at least 300 years earlier.

THE TWELVE DAYS OF CHRISTMAS

Traditional

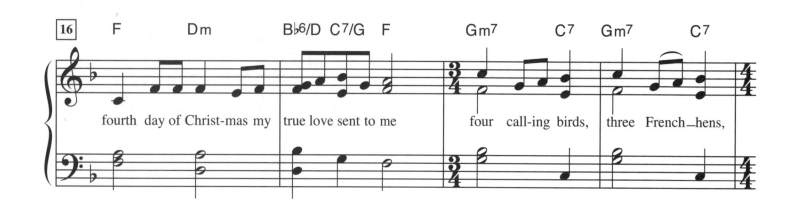

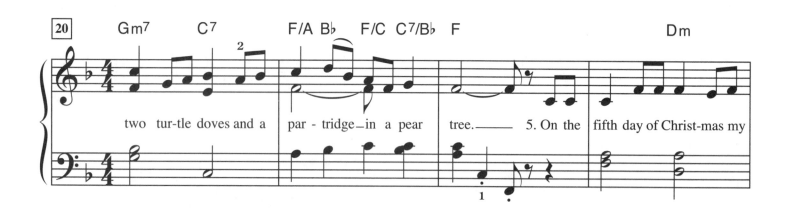

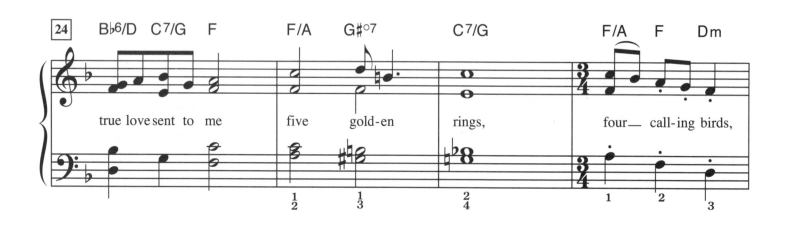

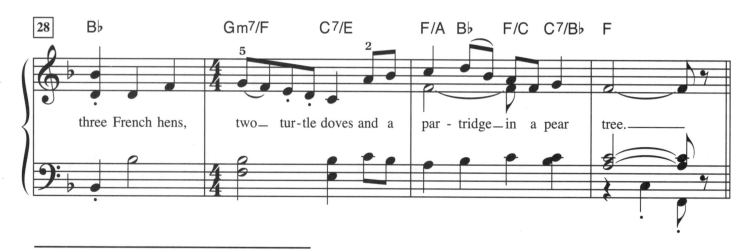

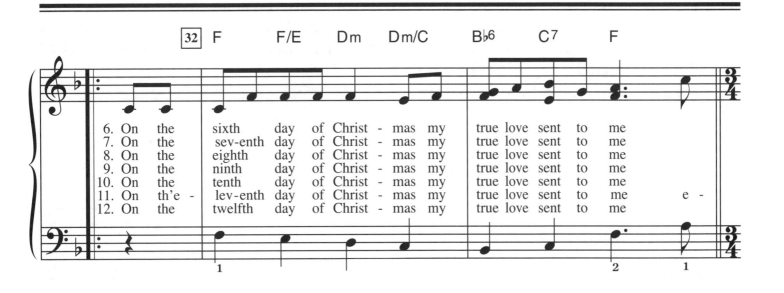

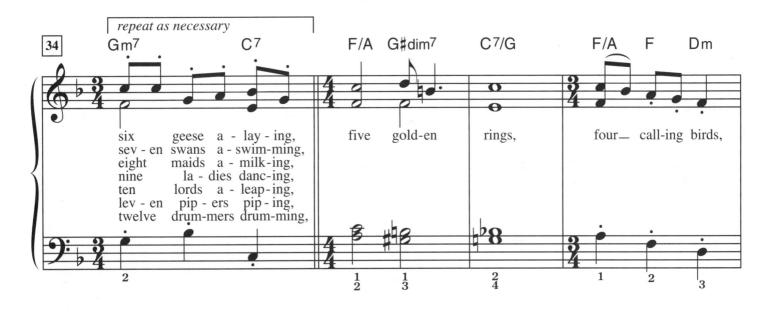

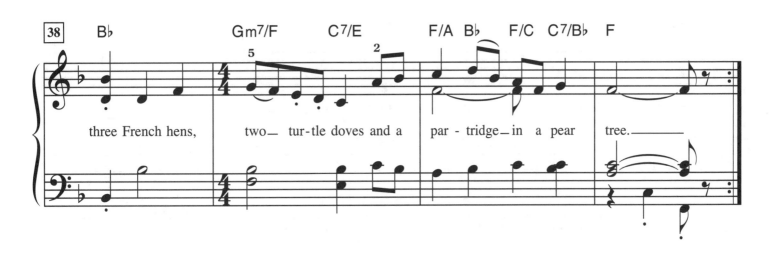

This piece is a product of songwriting team Mickey J. Addy (a composer of many Christmas favorites) and lyricist Carl Sigman, who is also responsible for dozens of hits including "What Now My Love," "It's All in the Game," "The Twelfth of Never," "Ebb Tide," "Pennsylvania 6-5000," and "Where Do I Begin (Love Story)."

THERE IS NO CHRISTMAS LIKE A HOME CHRISTMAS

Words by Carl Sigman
Music by Mickey J. Addy

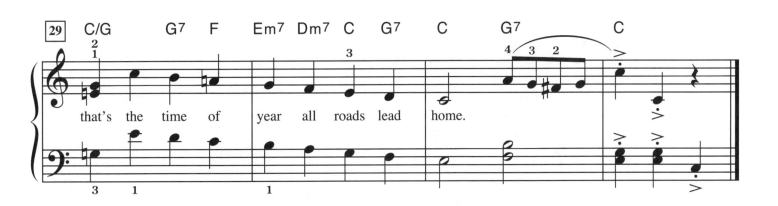

Victor Herbert and Glen MacDonough wrote their hit Broadway musical *Babes in Toyland*, which premiered in 1903. In 1934, a movie version featuring the comedy team of Laurel and Hardy brought the play to a much wider audience.

TOYLAND

Words by Glen MacDonough
Music by Victor Herbert

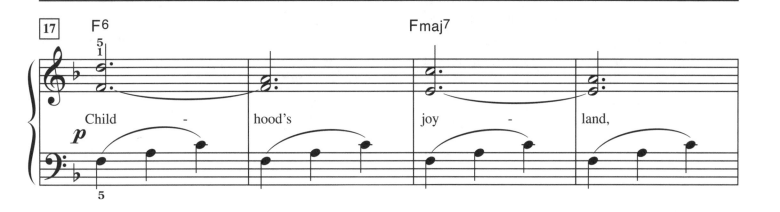

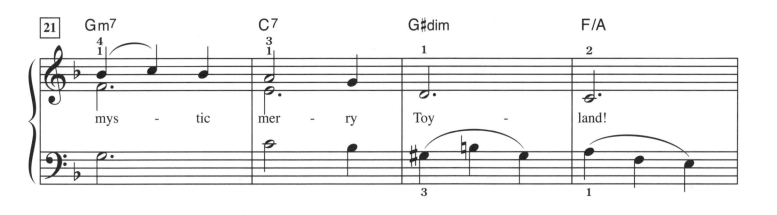

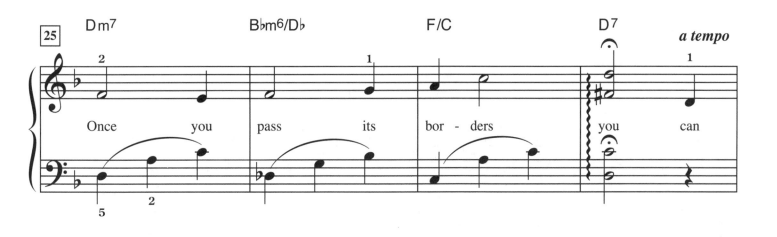

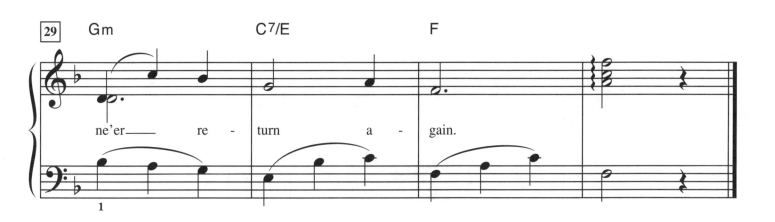

Ukrainian composer Mykola Leontovich portrayed the sound of Christmas bells in his choral work *Shchedryk*, which was first performed in Kiev in 1916. Twenty years later, composer and conductor Peter J. Wilhousky adapted Leontovich's music and added lyrics, creating the well-loved carol that we know today. The instrumental version of the piece is included here.

THE UKRAINIAN BELL CAROL

Music by
Mykola Leontovich

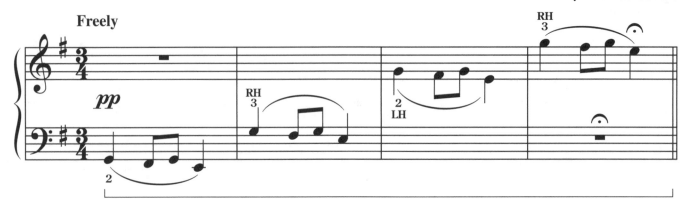

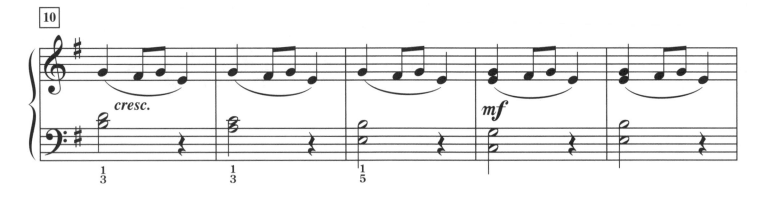

One of the reasons we picture Santa Claus as we do is because of C. C. Moore's famous 1822 poem, "A Visit from Saint Nicholas," also known as "The Night Before Christmas." In the poem are the eight tiny reindeer, the jolly old Santa Claus, and his rooftop method of delivering Christmas presents. *Up on the Housetop* was written a few years after Moore's poem became popular.

Up on the Housetop

Words and Music by
Benjamin Hanby

Originally a book by Dr. Seuss, *How the Grinch Stole Christmas* became an animated short in 1996, then a feature film in 2000, starring comedian Jim Carrey. Carrey had to wear so much makeup for the role that it took three hours for each day of filming to apply! Country singer Faith Hill had a hit record with this song, one of the highlights of the film.

WHERE ARE YOU CHRISTMAS

Words and Music by
James Horner, Will Jennings and Mariah Carey

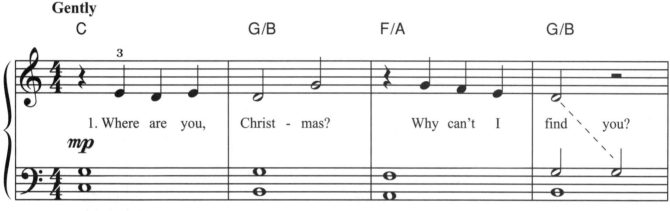

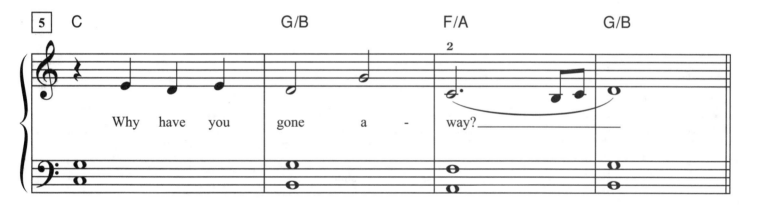

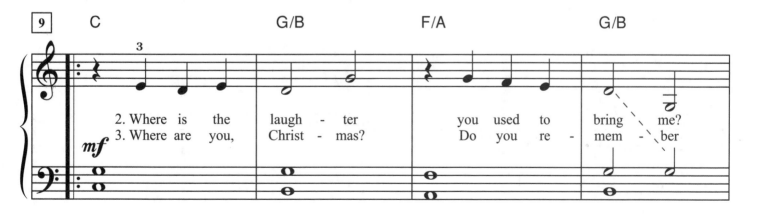

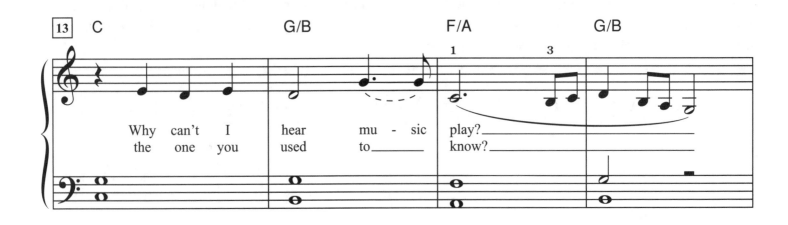

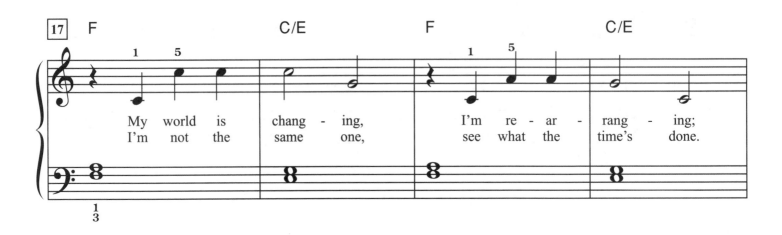

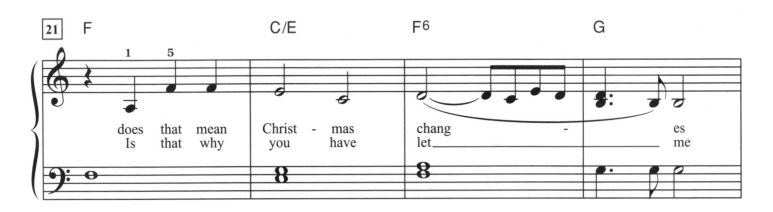

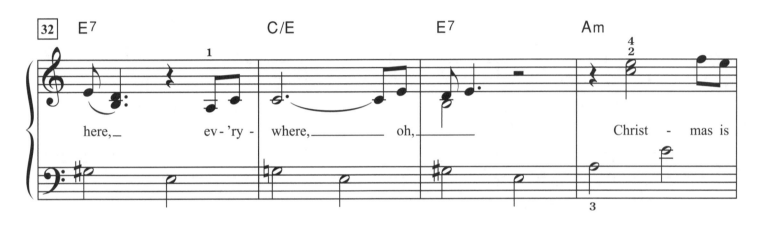

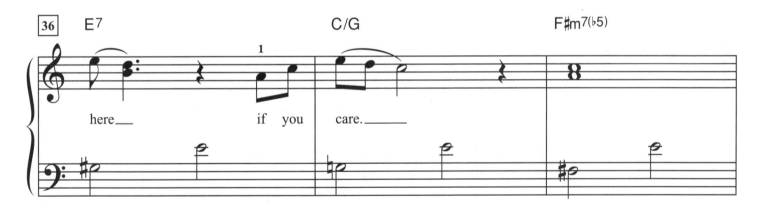

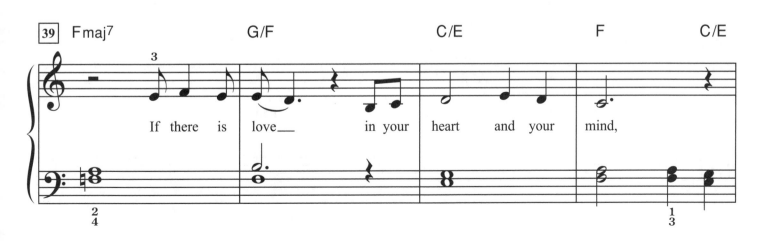

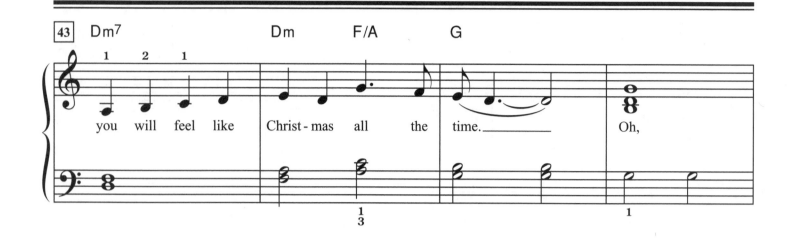

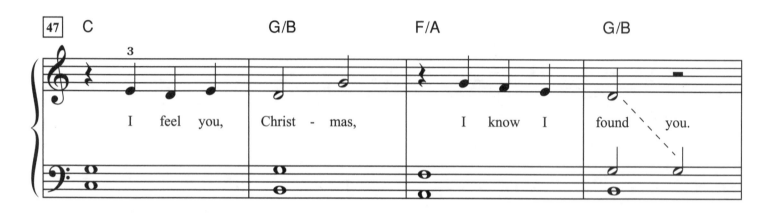

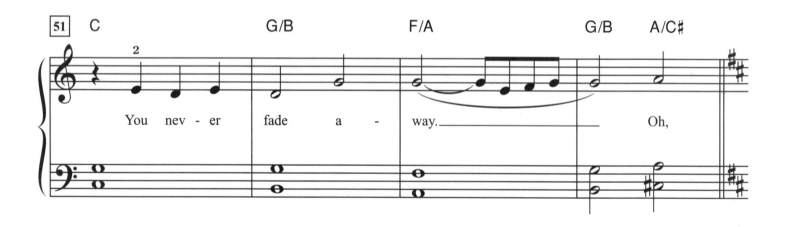

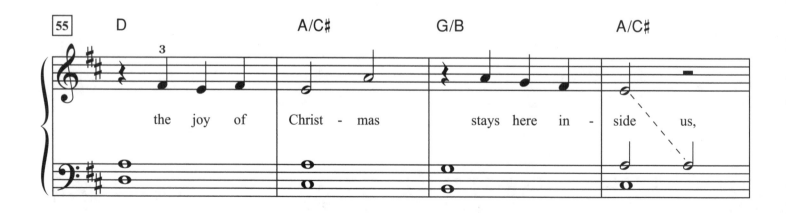

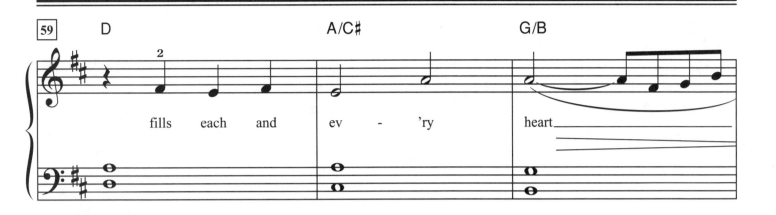

fills each and ev - 'ry heart

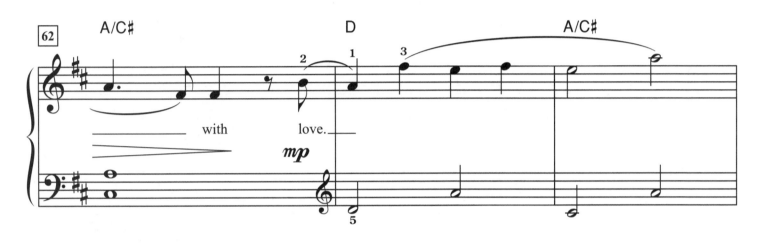

with love.

mp

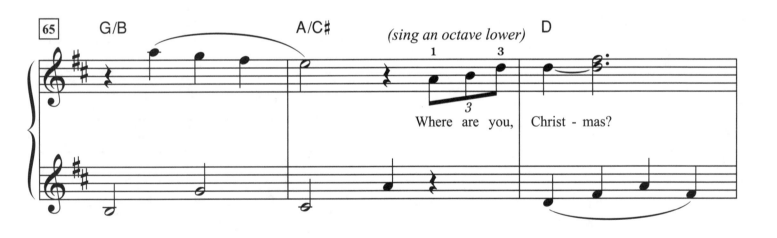

(sing an octave lower)

Where are you, Christ - mas?

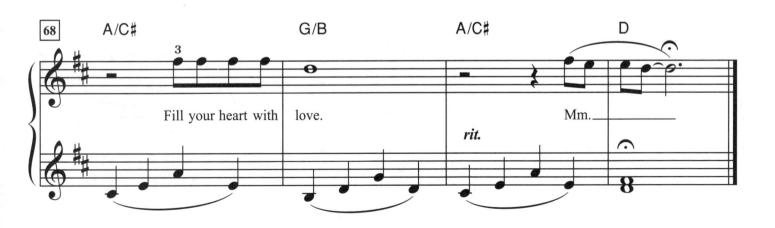

Fill your heart with love.

rit.

Mm.

American minister John Henry Hopkins wrote this carol for a Christmas pageant in 1857. At that time, he was criticized for calling the Wise Men "kings" (the Bible only mentions "men from the East"). The three kings are: Melchior, who brings gold to crown the new King; Gaspar, who brings frankincense, an aromatic gum used to make incense; and Balthasar, whose gift of myrrh (an aromatic gum used in burials) foretells the death of Jesus on the cross.

We Three Kings of Orient Are

Words and Music by
John Henry Hopkins, Jr.

2. Born a King on Bethlehem's plain,
   Gold I bring to crown Him again.
   King forever, ceasing never,
   Over us all to reign.
   (Chorus)

3. Frankincense to offer have I,
   Incense owns a Deity nigh.
   Pray'r and praising, all men raising,
   Worship Him, God most high.
   (Chorus)

4. Myrrh is mine, its bitter perfume
   Breathes a life of gathering gloom;
   Sorrowing, sighing, bleeding, dying,
   Sealed in the stone-cold tomb.
   (Chorus)

5. Glorious now behold Him arise,
   King and God and Sacrifice.
   Alleluia, Alleluia,
   Earth to heav'n replies.
   (Chorus)

In the late 1830s, England established a reliable, inexpensive postal service, which encouraged the writing of letters and cards, especially Christmas cards. The colorful cards often showed scenes of carolers, called *waits*, strolling snowy streets and singing for a bit of pudding or a cup of good cheer. This famous Christmas song was originally a waits carol, which became popular in mid-19th century England.

WE WISH YOU A MERRY CHRISTMAS

Traditional

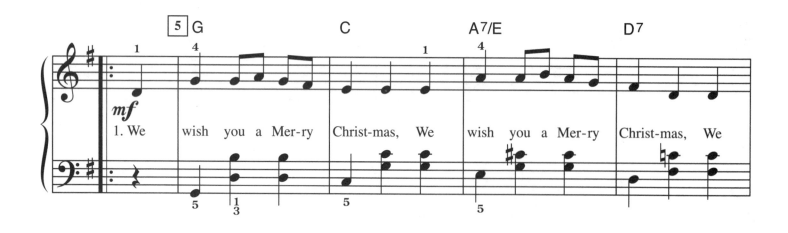

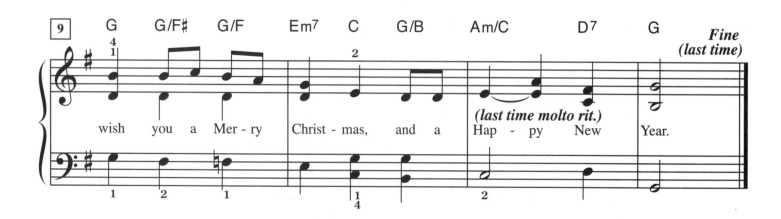

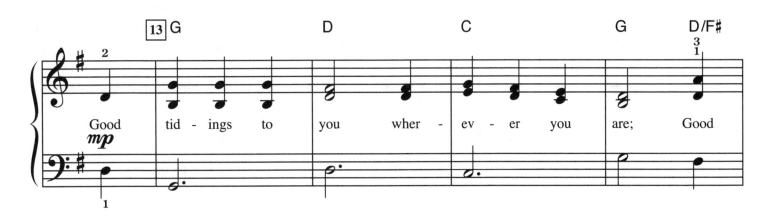

Good tid - ings to you wher - ev - er you are; Good

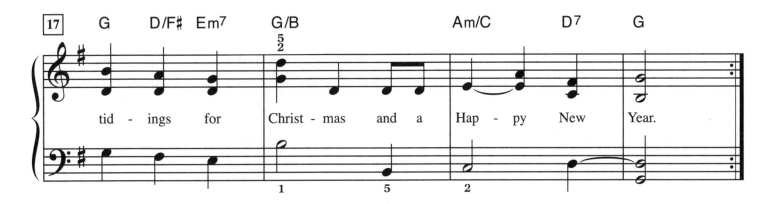

tid - ings for Christ - mas and a Hap - py New Year.

2. Oh, bring us a figgy pudding,
   Oh, bring us a figgy pudding,
   Oh, bring us a figgy pudding,
   And a cup of good cheer.
   Good tidings to you wherever you are;
   Good tidings for Christmas
   and a Happy New Year.

3. We won't go until we've got some,
   We won't go until we've got some,
   We won't go until we've got some,
   So bring some out here.
   Good tidings to you wherever you are,
   Good tidings for Christmas
   and a Happy New Year.

4. We wish you a Merry Christmas,
   We wish you a Merry Christmas,
   We wish you a Merry Christmas,
   and a Happy New Year.

Take a story by that master of nonsense—Dr. Seuss—combine it with the talents of rubber-faced comedian Jim Carrey, add songs by Albert Hague, and what do you have? Simply one of the most charming movies ever made about Christmas, *How the Grinch Stole Christmas*. Based on Dr. Seuss' children's book, *How the Grinch Stole Christmas*, the film tells the tale of a grumpy old hermit who finds the true meaning of Christmas.

WELCOME CHRISTMAS
(FROM *HOW THE GRINCH STOLE CHRISTMAS*)

Lyrics by Dr. Seuss
Music by Albert Hague

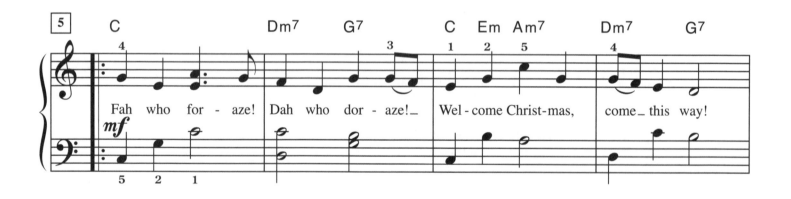

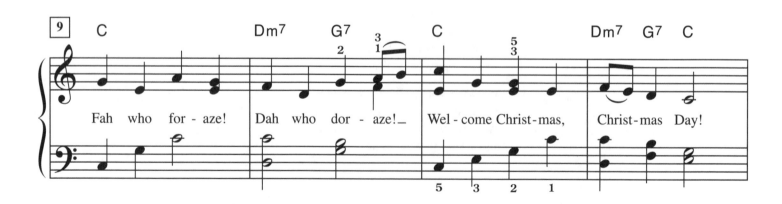

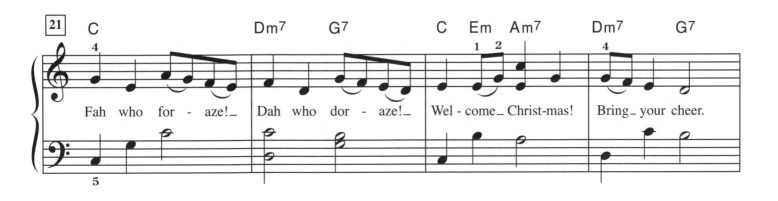

This beautiful carol uses the melody of the song *Greensleeves*, a song people have been singing, playing, and dancing to for over 400 years. Originally, the piece was played rather fast for dancing, but its real beauty was not revealed until someone had the inspiration to slow it down. In 1865, insurance man and sometime poet William Chatterton Dix wrote the words to the carol we sing today.

WHAT CHILD IS THIS?

Words by William Chatterton Dix
16th-century English Melody
("Greensleeves")

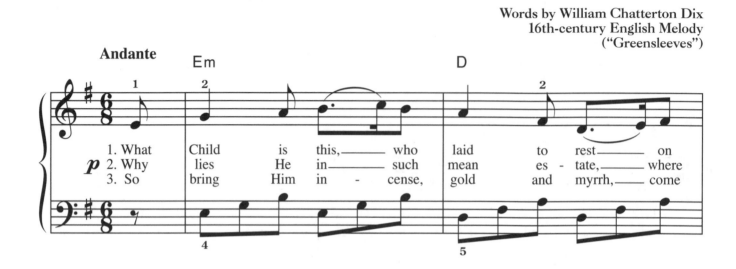

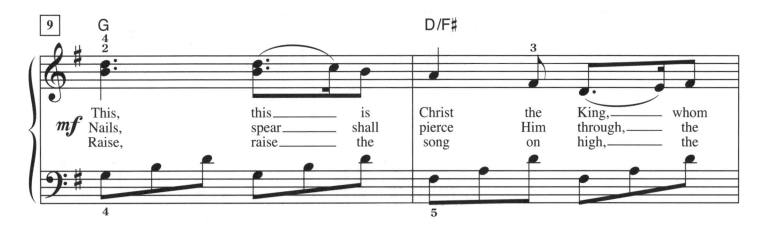

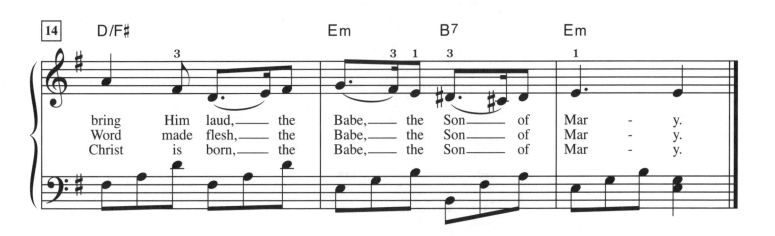

Who doesn't love snowmen and sleigh bells? Nobody, that's who! Written by music business pros Felix Bernard and Dick Smith, *Winter Wonderland* dates from 1934, but it took hit recordings by Perry Como and The Andrews Sisters in 1946 to establish the song as a Christmas standard.

WINTER WONDERLAND

Words by Dick Smith
Music by Felix Bernard

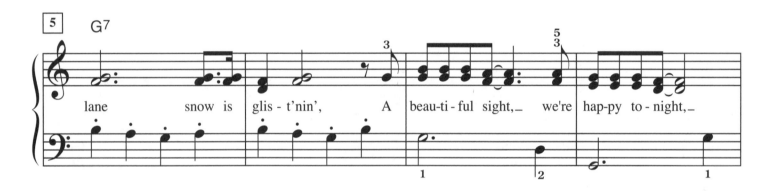

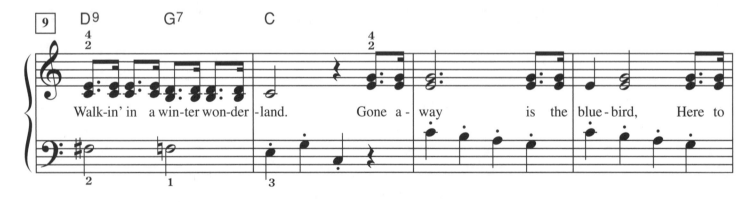